Introduction

Food dehydrating is an ancient method of food preservation that can be used for longer periods of time. It can be used to complement or replace freezing or canning.

It is simple, safe, and easy to dehydrate foods. You can dry everything at home, including banana chips, beef tenders, and fruit leathers.

Dehydration is a process that removes moisture from food products. This prevents bacterial growth.

The oldest method of food storage is dehydration. It was first used by humans to sun-dry vegetables. Sun-drying cuts allowed the North American Indians to store beef, preserve eggs from China, and dehydrate rice and fish from Japan.

Dehydrated fruits and vegetables aren't just for backpacking trekkers. Take a stroll through your local grocery store's healthy food section. You will find fruit chips and vegetarian options. These chips can be used for snacking or as a main dish with grilled sausage. Dry peppers can be used in winter soups, frozen pizzas, and you can also cut dried tomatoes into small pieces.

It is easy to learn how to dry fruits and vegetables. A dehydrator is a great investment, whether you're a fan of store-bought tortilla chips and adore apple slices. It is an easy, inexpensive and delicious way to preserve fresh food. It is especially useful if you have a Community Supported Agriculture box or garden.

The dairy industry is one of the largest producers of dehydrated foods. It produces large quantities of whole milk, condensed and coconut milk as well as eggs. Most milk products are spray-dried. This means that the product is commoditized into thin layers that make contact with warm air. The water content of almost all milk products can be removed almost immediately

Dehydrating food is simple and satisfying if you want to preserve your food, make healthier snacks, or plan for a hike in the future. The process of drying removes water slowly, but preserves nutrition and taste. It may be more affordable and healthier than precooked meals. This is important for travelers who want to reduce their weight and save space.

You will need a dehydrator for some recipes, but you can also cook certain foods using a lower oven. The process can be accelerated by a mandolin cutter, but it should be used with caution. It is not necessary to make delicious dehydrated foods. Even if you don't use a mandolin slicer, sharp knife skills can be very useful.

This book demonstrates the cycle of fruit and vegetable dehydration, with 100 recipes made from dehydrated foods.

Chapter 1: Getting Started with Dehydrating Foods

While dehydration was one of the first food storage methods, techniques for drying food have improved over time. Many people can save their food by dehydrating it at home.

To grow yeast, molds, and bacteria, water is essential. Food that is properly dehydrated will not allow microorganisms to grow. Also, food won't spoil. You can use dried fruits, vegetables, and fruit leathers as snacks, curries or casseroles. Hikers and climbers love dried products for their light weight, consistency and ease of preparation.

Continue reading to learn more about the basics of dehydration.

1.1   Process of Dehydration of Food

Dehydrated foods can be delicious, nutritious, portable, easy to transport, and user-friendly. A good drying process requires dry air, medium temperature, and proper movement. A variety of products can be dried using a dehydrator or refrigerator, microwave, or air-dryer.

Begin with food that is of good quality. Pretreatment is the process of blanching vegetables and preparing most fruits. It will take time for the food to dry completely. Food should be dried in a cool, dark place with sealed containers to keep insects away and dryness. Use the right combination of heat, low humidity, temperature current, to dry food products securely. You will need the following:

- Low Moisture. Low humidity ensures that moisture may transfer from the product to the air.
- Low-heat source. The warm air helps evaporate the moisture.
- Air travel. Air currents speed up drying.

Preparing Vegetables and Fruits for Drying
      Select a peak-season product.
Some people believe that dehydration is a way to make the most of items that have been thrashed, blistered or otherwise damaged. Drying can alter the taste of food, so make sure to continue enjoying top-quality foods that you love chewing.

- Wash, dry, and peel.

If you have the funds, purchase organic produce and give fruits and vegetables a quick, easy, or thorough wash. It is your choice whether you want to remove skins. However, skins will only get more difficult in texture.

- Cut thinly with a small knife or mandolin.

Choose pieces that are uniformly cut and approximately 1/8 to 1/4 inches wide. These pieces will dry simultaneously. As they dry, pieces will shrink. To ensure the best outcome, you can make your pieces a little thicker than you would like.

- Soak fruit in citrus water.

The stage can be done at your own discretion, but it is only for fruits that are brown (e.g. bananas and apples). Place the cut fruits in a tub with equal amounts of lime juice and cold tap water. Let them soak for ten minutes. Place the fruit in a bowl and let it drain on paper towels.

- Blanch vegetables in hot water.

This step is optional, but it is essential for starchy vegetables such as sweet snap peas or potatoes. To retain vibrant colors, simmer them for a few minutes.

It takes a long time to dry food. A dehydrator is required to dry foods for at least six hours. To bake, it takes at most 8 hours.

The following factors influence the time it takes to dehydrate:
    Food form.
    Cutting size.
- The food's humidity. Drying method.

Don't hurry the drying process by turning the oven up to high.

The food will be cooked outside, and dried inside. This is known as "case hardness". It can appear dry from the outside, but it is moist inside. It will eventually mold in reserve.

After Drying:

- Allow the fruit to cool for between 30-60 minutes before packing.
- Avoid packing too early or you risk retaining moisture.
- Do not wait too long, you might get moisture.

Test for Dryness

Dry fruit can be obtained when the moisture level is around 20%. Fruit that is warm will be more flexible. Let some portions cool down and then roll the fruit over to check for any signs of bind. The berries should rattle when placed in a container. Keep the fruit cool until it is dry. Do not let the fruit sit out in order to retain moisture. The drug can then be packed.

Dehydrated vegetables should be crisp when dried. When broken in half, they should be "split". At this moisture level, no conditioning is necessary.

Conditioning

The final stage of drying dried foods is conditioning them after pasteurizing or drying. To preserve berries, place the chilled liquid in a glass container and toss it every day for 7-10 working days. If moisture is present, bring it back to your dehydrator. After conditioning, package of dried food should be kept for ten days. Remember to keep foods high in vitamin A and C out of direct sunlight during processing. Conditioning stabilizes moisture.

Because food is deficient in nutrients, it is shrinking rapidly. This should be considered when deciding how much produce to grow. One pound of apples (before cutting) yields approximately one cup of dried apple slices. Finely sliced foods can encourage even dehydration. However, it is important to not cut too many pieces as they could get lost in the rehydration process.

1.2 Methods and Procedures of Drying Food

Below are some of the most common methods and techniques for dehydrating fruits and vegetables.

Sun Drying

Because of its high sugar and acid content, the fruit can be dried in the sun. Vegetables and meats are not allowed to dry in the sun. Vegetables are low in sugar and high in acidity. This can increase spoilage risks. Because meats are high in protein, they can be adapted to bacterial growth in hot weather. For drying in the sun, dry, warm and breezy periods are ideal.

It is recommended that you keep your food at 86 degrees F. It takes many days to dry food outdoors. Sun drying can be dangerous because of the extreme heat. The humidity level can also be a problem in the South. Sun drying requires moisture levels below 60 percent. These ideal conditions are almost impossible to find when the fruit is mature.

You can dry fruit in the sun on glass trays and wood dowel rods. These displays are safe for food contact. Steel, fiberglass coated with Teflon or plastic are the best options for screens. This is a metal galvanized fabric that is coated with zinc or cadmium. These materials can oxidize and leave harmful traces on food. You should also discourage the screening of aluminum and copper. Copper destroys vitamin C and causes oxidation. Aluminum aims to become discolored and corroded.

Trays can be made from some woods. Greenwood, fir and oak are not suitable for making trays. These woods can corrode, discolor or cause food to lose its flavor. To improve air circulation around the product, place trays on boards. Because the surface might be too wet, it is best to place shelves or screens on concrete patios.

The temperature range is improved by the sun's reflection onto the metal. To protect the produce from birds and insects, cover the trays with cheesecloth. Protect the fruits that are drying in direct sunlight at night. The cool night breeze can condense and bring humidity back to the product, slowing down the drying process.

Solar Drying

Solar drying is a current attempt to increase sun-drying. It uses the sun to heat up. The foil covering within the dehydrator heats up. Ventilation speeds up drying times, which can lead to food contamination and mold growth.

Pasteurization

You must take care of dried vine beans and solar-dried fruit to kill any insects or larvae. They may eat the dried fruit until they die. Two methods of pasteurization are recommended:

1. Chill approach - Cover the food with plastic bags that are freezer-safe and place in a freezer at or below 0 degrees F. Keep the food there for at least 48 hours.
2. Oven technique - Place the fresh produce in one layer on a tray, or in a large pan. Put the fresh produce in a oven for about half an hour at 160°F. After any of these treatments, the dried fruit can be fully prepared and stored.

Drying Foods Indoors

Most foods can be dried indoors using modern dehydrators, convection ovens or traditional ovens. Because they don't allow for air flow, microwave ovens are not recommended for dehydrating herbs.

Food Dehydrators

A food dehydrator can be described as a small electrical appliance that allows indoor drying of fruits.

A food dehydrator features an electric heat feature and air ventilation fan and vents. The dehydrators can dry food at 140 degrees F. They are relatively new brands and are sold in stores, home delivery catalogs, online food markets, plant catalogs and garden supply shops. Based on the functionality, prices range between $40 and $350. You can buy more trays later, or you can extend the versions. A half-bushel contains approximately 12 square feet drying area.

Oven Drying

Anyone who has an oven can use it as a dehydrator. A dehydrator can be made from an oven by using heat, humidity, and airflow. A oven can be used to dry jerkies and fruit leathers or fruit chips. It can also be used to store excess products like celery and mushrooms. The oven is essential for daily cooking. However, it may not be enough to preserve large amounts of garden produce. Because the oven does not have a fan, drying is slower than in dehydrators. Some convection furnaces do have fans. It takes two times as long to dry food in an oven than in a dehydrator. Because the oven is not as efficient as a dehydrator it takes more resources.

Homemade Solar Dryer

Use Your Oven: First, check the toggle to make sure it is able to show as low as 140°F. You can still cook your food if the oven doesn't have this feature. You can also use a thermometer for testing the temperature setting to "high". For air ventilation, keep the oven door open from 2-6 inches. A ventilator can be placed outside the oven's front door to improve circulation.

Note: This is not a good idea for children who live in a home with young children. Because the door is open, temperatures can fluctuate.

A thermometer placed next to the food will give you a precise reading. Change the temperature knob to reach 140°F. To reach the oven's edges, drying trays should be small enough. Cake cooling racks placed on top   of cookie sheets work well for certain products. The shelves should be at least 2 to 3 inches from the tray for air circulation.

1.3   Tools and Equipment Required

When food is exposed to low temperatures, dehydration occurs. This is a long-term process of water removal. These are some things that you might need for this process:

- An electronic dehydrator: This system dries your foods in an insulated space, while hot air circulates throughout your food. Here are two examples of a dehydrator.

  - An oven that is conventional: This oven can be used to dry food before you invest in an electric dehydrator. It will keep the temperature at a lower level and can withstand a day without it.

  - Oven thermometer: A thermometer will let you know if your oven temperature drops low enough to dry fresh produce, but not cook it.
- Shelves and trays: These are used to hold your fresh produce while it is being dried. They have an electric dehydrator included. Using meshlined frames or baking plates for oven-drying. Clean screens are required for sun-drying, clean cheesecloth to prevent thirsty insects off the product as it dehydrates. Cutting Board & Sharp Knife.
- You will also need other products: There are many types of bowls/utensils and plates. It is easy to understand the essential kitchenware you need for your daily cooking. These items will also be useful for dehydrated trips.

1.4 Fruits, Vegetables and their Required Drying Time

Drying times are not a science. It can vary depending on the method used and the fruits and vegetables. For vegetables, it can take 4 to 12 hours for them to dry, while fruits can take 6 to 20, but drying can take days if they are large or small.

What would you do if your vegetables and fruits were dried? Like a raisin fruit, they should be flexible and soft. For vegetables, they should be firm and crunchy. However, there are exceptions like tomatoes which can remain leathery if dried.

Here are some fruits and vegetables that are commonly found with their dryness checked.

Apples

Slice into 1/8 inch strips or circles by peeling and de-seeding. Pre-treat by dipping for 2 minutes.

Dryness Test: Soft, elastic, and creamy skin. There should be no moisture inside the slice.

Bananas

Peel and cut into 1/4" pieces. Mix 1/2 cup pineapple juice with 1/4 cup honey.
Dryness Test: Soggy, chewy, and caramel-like in colour.

Cherries

Take out the pits and stems. If the fruit is still juicy, drain for at least an hour.

Dryness Test: Very gluey, but leathery.

Grapevines

You can leave it as is, but you should discard the stems. To crack the skins, dip them in simmering water.

Dryness Test: Soft and dark brown.

Pears

Take out the seed and any woody tissue, and then peel it. Cut into 1/4 inch circles, squares, quarters, or eighths. Dip in the solution to pretreat.

Dryness Test: Leathery. You will feel springy.

Pineapple

Cut, core, and then peel 1/2 inch thick.
Dryness Test: Flexible to touch and spongy.

Plums

This is also true for prunes. Freestone varieties can be used.

Dryness Test: Flexible, leathery.

Red and Lima beans

Just until tender, steam for 15-20 minutes.
Dryness Test: When struck, it crumbles.

Broccoli

Cut 1/2 inch strips in long directions. Steam for 10 minutes or until tender but firm.

Dryness Test: Quite dark green, Brittle.

Cabbage

Cut into strips about 1/8 inches thick. Steam for 5-10 minutes or until the mixture is firm but not hard. Evenly extended to a length of not more than 1 inch. Use lemon juice to pre-treat.

Dryness Test: Crunchy, pale or greenish-yellow.

Carrots

Scrape. Split crosswise 1/8-inch in width, or dice 1/4-inch into pieces. Wash little parts, 3 minutes before steaming (or shredding). Place in thin layers on trays.

Dryness Test: Very fragile and a dark orange color.

Celery

Cut the stalk in half and remove the leaves. The water should be boiled for at least 1 to 2 minutes or until it is tender. Continue to stir the water while drying it.

Dryness Test: Quite crude.

Corn

Husk to be cut. Blanch whole ears for 9 minutes. For medium-to-full kernels, blanch for 3-5 mins. After blanching, remove corn from the ground.

Dryness Test: When hit, it crumbles.

Greens

Take out the rough stems. Steam for 5 minutes or until tender. Spread 1/4 inch deep leaves, such as spinach, onto the pad.

Dryness Test: Very dark green Crunchy.

Onions

Peel and cut the rings into 1/8 inch. Blanch for one minute. Steam when it is dry.
Dryness Test: Quite flippant.

Green peas

Steam the peas for 3 to 4 minutes or until tender. While drying, stir.
Dryness Test: When pressed, it will make a squeak.

Peppers and pimentos (of any type)

Divide bars or circles into 1/2-inch pieces. Remove seeds. Turn on the steamer for 10 minutes. Spread rings in two layers. Do not spread stripes more than 1/2 inch.
Dryness Test: Flexible.

Squash and Zucchini

Cut 1/4 inch slices without peeling. Steam for 6 minutes, or until soft.

Dryness Test: Leathery to yellow. Fragile.

Tomatoes (only meaty
sorts):
Put in boiling water for one minute. Cut off the end of the head and slice 1/8 inch thick.

Dryness Test: Leathery, intense red.

Chapter 2: Storing and Preserving Dried Food

Dehydration is not only time-saving but also extremely safe.

Dehydrated foods not only preserve their vitamin and mineral content but also have a long shelf-life. Participants in the process are guaranteed to make progress by following these simple instructions.

Dried fruit and vegetables can be preserved for up to five years, while vegetables can last up to ten. Non-meat products can be stored in plastic bags or ice bags, with the air removed. For long-term survival, vacuum-sealing with an oxygen-absorber works well. Keep it in a cool, dark place.

Use logic to avoid eating stale food.

Continue reading for more information about drying food and how to use it.

2.1 Storing and Preserving Your Dried Foods Properly

Drying reduces the food's moisture. This means that bacteria, yeast, and mold cannot grow and ruin the product. While drying can delay the process of food ripening, it doesn't stop enzyme activity. The product will lose weight and become lighter as the moisture is removed. When the food product is used, it returns water to the product.

Food can be dried in the sun, oven, or food dehydrator if it has the right combination of humidity, high temperatures, and air pressure. The heat allows the water to evaporate and dry out. Low humidity allows for easy moisture transfer from the product to its surface. The warm atmosphere pushes the food away from the air, which accelerates drying.

Dryness Test and Cooling before Storage

When vegetables are brittle, they become crispier and when fruits are dried, they become leathery. It takes between 30-50 minutes to cool the food after it has dried. The long cooling period allows moisture to return to the food from the atmosphere.

Choose the Correct Package to Store

Proper storage and handling of food will prevent it from being eaten by rats and insects. It seals out air, which preserves nutrients.

Use metal containers, glass bottles, and boxes with lids that are securely fastened or vapor-proof.

Screw lids and covers for glass bottles can be used to prevent ingestion by insects. However, the jars might not have to be dried. While heavy-duty bags can be sealed, they are not rodent or pest proof.

Inspect the containers to make sure there is no moisture within 7-10 days. If the product is still moist, take it out and dry it again. Throw away any food that has gone mouldy.

Dehydrated Food Shelf-life

- Based on storage conditions, dried foods last for 4-12 months.
- Retain in cold, dry, dark corners.
-

For greater efficiency, store below 60 F. It is best to keep dry goods out of reach of the refrigerator.

Cool the food completely after drying it. Next, transfer the food into sterile containers that are resistant to moisture or vapor. If they have lids that are secure, glass bottles, metal cans, and bins for freezing are all great containers for food. Plastic freezer bags can be used, but they aren't rodent- or insect-proof. Avoid contacting metal with sulphured fruit. Keep the fruit in a container until you can place them in a container made of metal. For one year, the dried fruit can be stored at 60 degrees F and 80 degrees F for six months. Dry vegetables can keep for half as long as fruit. Fruit leathers can be kept at room temperature up to one month. To preserve dry foods longer, please place them in the freezer.

2.2 Use of Dried Foods

Dried fruits can be used as delicious treats, or soaked for at least 1-2 hours and then used in your favorite dishes. For snacks, bananas, pears and apples can be dried thoroughly.

Produced from perfectly ripe fruits, fruit leathers make nutritious snacks.

Most dehydrated vegetables can be refashioned into hot food, sauces or filling ingredients. You can simply add dried vegetables to a soup or curry and let them sit for a while before rehydrating.

To rehydrate or restore leafy vegetables, boil water in a saucepan. Before frying, soak root crops and seeds, such as cabbage, green beans, peas, and peas, in warm water.

Let the cold water sit for 30 to 90 minutes. Fill it with boiling water for 20-60 seconds. Let it simmer, stirring occasionally, until it boils.

Advice: If the product needs to be soaked for more than two hours, freeze it. This will prevent bacterial growth.

Two cups of reconstituted vegetables are equivalent to one cup of dehydrated vegetables. Reconstituted fruits and vegetables can be considered fresh.

You can use dried vegetables directly:
- You can eat a dried slice of vegetables as crispy vegetable chips for sauces.
- Dehydrated vegetables can be added in curries or soups depending on the water in the curry or soup for rehydration.
- Cut and dehydrate green pepper, cabbage, celery, and green onions for immediate use during the year.
- Create your onion powder by dehydrating slices of onion into the mixer until crispy and powdered.

- To use in sandwiches, carrot cake, stews, soups or risottos, grate the carrots.

2.3 Benefits of Drying Food At Home

Dehydrated foods can be nutritious, light, tasty, portable, and simple to store. Dehydrated foods require less energy than those that are stored in cans. Also, the storage space is much smaller than that required for canning containers and jars.

The nutritional content of the meal is not affected by drying. Vitamin A can be preserved after drying. However, vitamin A is sensitive to light so food containing it should not be stored in direct sunlight. Vitamin A is found in large quantities in dark green and yellow vegetables such as sweet potatoes, cabbage, carrots and cabbage. Heat exposure can cause vitamin C to be damaged. Vitamin C quality can be improved by pretreatment with orange, pineapple, and lemon juices.

Dehydrated fruits, vegetables and other foods are high in fiber and carbohydrate and less fat. This gives them safe nutritional options. Dry fruits have a higher carbohydrate content than fresh fruit, so serving sizes are smaller. The USDA's American Dietary Guidelines states that a half cup of dehydrated fruit equals one cup of fresh fruit. To reduce high blood glucose levels, people with diabetes might consider smaller portions when making snacks or meals.

Other benefits include:
- Save some cash. You will be able to enjoy your own garden's benefits, and it will also encourage you to take advantage of the grocery store's specials.
- Less waste. Bear in mind that dehydrating food is single-time expenditure. Canned products should be consumed immediately until sealed, but dry food containers may be sealed regularly, items added or removed, then

sealed again with no adverse effects on the products. Easy food. Dry products are super easy since they can be consumed exactly the way they are.

- Store more significant numbers. With much less room, you can preserve more food than dried or frozen items.
- Improved flavor.   Gives you an organic "strong" flavor in   snacks.
- Nutrition. Retains more nutrient content than food, which is frozen or canned.

2.4 List of Top Fruits and Vegetables to Dehydrate

Many foods can be dried at home, with the exception of high-fat meats and other high-fat foods. You can cook most vegetables and meat before you dehydrate them, unlike berries. These can be turned into meals until you have a variety of dried ingredients. You can cook any food, even soups and risottos, and then dehydrate them. This reduces planning and allows for the blending of flavors.

Allow multiple products to be dehydrated simultaneously for productivity. They will need to have the same drying temperature.

Here are the top fruits and veggies that you can dehydrate at home:

1. Bananas.
Make fun dried banana coins for kids to enjoy as a healthy snack. To prevent any discoloration, peel the bananas. Then, cut into disks of 1/8 to 1/4 inches thick. Let them sit for 10 minutes in lemon juice. Dehydrate the bananas for 6-10 hours at 135°F or bake at 200°F for 5-7 hours, depending on the manufacturer's instructions.

2. Strawberries.
Dehydrated sweet strawberries and granola work well together. Cut strawberries in quarters to 1/4 inch width. If they are small, you can also cut them in half. You can either dehydrate them for 7-15 hours at 135°F or bake them in the oven for 5-7 hours at 200°F, depending on the manufacturer's instructions.

3. Apples.

Dry apples make a great snack. It is easy to dehydrate apples. To prevent discoloration, you can cut the core of the apples and then place them in the citrus bath for 10 to 15 minutes. You can either dehydrate the fruit for 7-15 hours at 135°F or bake it in the oven for 6-8 hours at 200°F, depending on the manufacturer's instructions.

4. Pineapple.

Grand prize for dehydrated pineapple Cut the top off the pineapple, then cut 1/4 to 1/2 inch into the middle. Finally, remove the core. You can either dehydrate the product for between 10-18 hours at 135°F or bake it in the oven for 8-10 hours at 200°F, depending on the instructions of the supplier.

5. Mangoes.

Mango strips taste like sunshine Take out the flesh from the mango and cut it into strips about one-and-a-half inches in length. You can either dehydrate the mango for 7-15 hours at 135°F or bake it in the oven for 6-8 hours at 200°F, depending on the manufacturer's instructions.

6. Tomatoes.

For pasta night, dehydrated or sun-dried tomatoes are great. Top tomatoes can be cut in 1/4 inch slices or split into two pieces. You can either dehydrate the tomatoes for between 5-9 hours at 155°F or bake them in the oven for between 4-6 hours at 200°F, depending on the manufacturer's instructions.

7. Zucchini.

One summer squash can be saved by dehydration. Slice the tops and ends one-half to one-half inches deep. You can either dehydrate the fruit for seven to eleven hours at 125 degrees F or bake it in the oven for five hours at 200 degrees F.

8. Sugar Snap Peas.

Peas dehydrated make a great snack, even better than French fries. Cut the strings and marinate for a few minutes in hotwater. Then, shake them in an ice-cream bucket. Dehydrate at 125 degrees F for 5-13 hours or at 200 degrees F for 4-6hrs, depending on the instructions of the manufacturer.

9. Sweet Potatoes.

Although they won't be as crispy as deep-fried chips or sweet potatoes, dry sweet potatoes will always be delicious. Slice the sweet potatoes 1/4 inch thick. After marinating for a few minutes, place in a bowl of hot water. Finally, shake in an ice-cream bucket. You can either dehydrate the sweet potatoes for 7-11 hours at 120°F or bake them in the oven for 6-8 hours at 200°F, depending on the manufacturer's instructions.

10. Bell Peppers.

You can use dehydrated peppers to make soup mixes that include confetti colors. Cut or dice the peppers 1/4 inch deep. Dehydrate at 125 degrees F for 4-8 hours or at 200 degrees F for 4-6, depending on the instructions of the manufacturer.

Chapter 3: Breakfast Recipes with Dehydrated Foods

Dehydrated food ingredients can be used to make a variety of breakfasts with a twist.

Discover delicious and healthy breakfast options that you can make at home or outdoors.

3.1 Breakfast Recipes

Dehydrated Powdered Eggs
Ingredients:

- 5 eggs

Instructions:

- Break eggs into a bowl.
- Mix the eggs until they are almost frothy.
-
- Place the eggs carefully onto the fruit leather plate of the dehydrator. The eggs should be dried at 140°F for 8-10 hours until they are dry and flaky. The egg pieces will become sticky and may be able to scratch off quickly, drying completely without sticking to the plate. Keep the sticky part in place if they are already sticky.

- Shift the dried egg pieces to a zip lock bag and put half to 1 hour in the freezer.
- Take them out from the freezer and combine them until fully powdered in a food processor. They are not dried enough if they cling to the edges. Put for some extra time back into the dehydrator. Store in the freezer for later use.

To Rehydrate:

- Mix 1 tbsp. + 1 tsp. of water for each egg straight into the zip lock bag, so that you might discard it afterward without thinking about polluting the cooking utensils with raw egg.
- Let stay for another 5 minutes, add the water a bit faster if required.

3 Mushroom Risotto

Ingredients:

- Half cup dehydrated cooked rice
- Half cup dried mushrooms (Portobello porcini)
- Vegetable bouillon cube 1/4 Dried parsley 1/2
- tsp.
-
- Dried thyme 1/4 tsp.
- Salt and Pepper
Freezer-dried Parmesan cheese 2 tbsp.

Instructions:

- Mix mushrooms, rice, dried herbs, and bouillon cube.
- Mix the ingredients in a frying pan. Add 1 cup water to the pan and stir. Even if you sit for 10 minutes, it is still a lot.
- Over medium heat, bring the mix to boil. Add salt and pepper.
- Cook the mixture, stirring constantly until it is almost completely
- drained. Turn off the heat and cover with Parmesan cheese.

Notes: Use vegan Parmesan cheese for vegan type.

Brown Rice Cereal

Ingredients:

- Dehydrated cooked rice, (coarse powder) 1/4 cup Full
- cream milk powder 2 tbsp.
- Brown sugar 1 tbsp.
- Ground cinnamon 1/4 tsp.
- Diced, freeze-dried apples 2 tbsp.
- Ground flaxseed 1 teaspoon
- Ghee 1 teaspoon.

Instructions:

- Mix all dry ingredients.
- In a saucepan, boil 1 1/2 cups water.

- In the Brown Rice Cereal mixture, add hot water.
- Stir well, close the container, and let it sit for around 5 minutes in a warm place. Add ghee.

Frittata
Ingredients:
- Powdered whole eggs 6 tbsp.
- 1 tbsp full cream milk powder.
- Tomatoes, chopped 2 tbsp.
- Dried oregano 1/4 tsp.
- Dried marjoram 1/4 tsp.
- Sea Salt
- Pepper
- 1 tbsp olive oil or ghee.
- Chorizo 20 grams
- Shallot 1
Frozen-dried Parmesan cheese 1 tbsp.

Instructions:

- Mix milk, powdered eggs, dried herbs, and tomatoes.
- Mix egg mixture with 3/4 cup of water.
-
- Salt and pepper to your taste. Then, put it aside.
-

In a saucepan, heat the ghee.

Remove the chorizo from the bones and chop the onions. Place the chopped onions in a saucepan and cook until tender.

- Turn over the eggs pounded, and then cover with a top. Reduce heat to moderate.
- Continue cooking, about 10 minutes, until the frittata center is formed.
- Turn off heat and cover with Parmesan.

Fruity Dream
Ingredients:

- Freeze-dried strawberries 10 grams.
- Diced, freeze-dried apples 10 grams.
- Sliced bananas frozen-dried 10 grams.
- Almond flour 1 tbsp.
- Ground flaxseed 1 tbsp.
- Chopped pecans, 30 grams.
- Coconut milk powder 2 Tbsp.

Instruction:

- Mix all the ingredients in a zip-lock bag.
- Boil one-and-a-half cups of water.
-

Add hot water to the container and garnish with Fruity Dream.

- Stir well, shut the container, and let it sit for around 5 minutes in a warm place.

Raw Buckwheat Porridge

- Raw buckwheat grouts 1 cup
- Almonds 1/2 cup
- Almond milk 1 cup

Instructions:

- Pour grouts of buckwheat and almonds into different dishes, fill with water, leave for at least 1 hour, or ideally overnight.
- Move the saturated buckwheat to a colander. Rinse thoroughly, and then drain.
- Add all ingredients in a processor, and blend until creamy at high rpm.
- Distribute the buckwheat porridge on non-stick layer or parchment paper-lined dehydrator trays. Dry for 6-8 hours at 130F/52C, until stiff. Allow it to sit at room temperature, either use a hand blender to jerk the

- Porridge bark can be cut into small pieces or crushed into powder. Divide into four equal portions (approximately 55g/2.3 oz). Each.

- Add your preferred sugar substitute (stevia paste, brown sugar) and toppings (super food mix freeze-dried fruits berries, peanut butter paste, and nuts) to a portion of porridge.
- Pour 1/4 cup hot or cold water over dried fresh buckwheat porridge into the bowl.
- Mix well, cover the bowl and let your breakfast rehydrate fully for around 5 minutes.

Keto Porridge

Ingredients:
- Coconut flour 2 tbsp.
- Ground flaxseed 2 tbsp.
- Coconut milk powder 2 Tbsp.
-
- Chia seeds 1 tbsp.
- Swerve sweetener 2 tsp.
- Ghee 1 tsp.

Chopped pecans, 10 grams

Instructions:

- Mix ground Chia seeds, flax seeds, coconut flour, sweetener, and coconut milk powder.
- Add 1/2 cup water in Keto Porridge and mix properly.
- Place the pot on the burner, and heat the porridge.
-
-

- Cook on low heat for 3-4 minutes or until the mixture is smooth. Mix in
- the ghee, and toss with the pecans.

Dehydrated Yogurt

Ingredients:

- Regular Yogurt

Instructions:

- To avoid spoiling, use regular yogurt with low-fat value (3 percent or less). You may add sweeteners and taste/aroma additives.
- Place the yogurt in an even, light coating (about 1/8 "thick) on a dehydrator tray lined with a non-stick layer or parchment paper. At 135F/57C, dehydrate for around 6-8 hours, unless thoroughly dried and brittle.
- Flip the tray every few hours, and turn the yogurt bark midway through the dehydrating process.
- Take out from the dryer and allow it to cool.
- You can freeze it by securing it with a suction seal.
-

Dehydrated yogurt can be kept at room temperature for up to a week if it is not refrigerated.

- Crush dehydrated bits of yogurt using a hand grinder into powder form.

Chocolate Almond Smoothie

Ingredients:

- Banana 1
- Wheat berries/rolled oatmeal 2 tbsp.
- Almond/peanut butter 1 tbsp.
- Ground flaxseed 1 tsp.
- Cocoa 1 tsp.
- Almond milk 3/4 cup

Instructions:

- Add all ingredients together in a blender.
  Do a quick cycle to get slick and foamy.

  Layer the parchment or non-stick sheet over the dehydrator tray.

- Dehydrate for 6-12 hours at 115F/46C, until thoroughly dried and hard.
- Allow to cool to room temperature after drying.
-
-
- Blend the dry smoothie mixture into a fine powder using a grinder.
- Place the smoothie concentrate in a mug.
Mix well, then add 1/3 cup of water.

Allow them to stand for five minutes and then let them rehydrate.

Pumpkin Chia Overnight Oats Ingredients:

- Quick-cooking oats 3 tbsp.
- Pumpkin powder 2 tbsp.
- Coconut milk powder 2 Tbsp.
-
- Chia seeds 1 tbsp.
- Brown sugar 1 tsp.
- Pumpkin spice 1/2 tsp.

Instructions:

- Mix all the components in a zip lock container of medium lengths.
- Place the oat mixture in a container or bottle.
-
- To make dust, use 3/4 cup of water.

Seal the container well and let it sit for at least 4 hours.

Pumpkin Pancakes

Ingredients:

- Pancake batter mix, 100 grams 3.53oz
- Pumpkin powder 2 tbsp.

Ghee, for frying.

Instructions:

- Mix the pumpkin powder and pancake batter combination in a zip-lock bag.
- In the pancake batter mix, add half to 2/3 cup water.
- Mix the ingredients in a bowl. Cover the bag and seal it.
-
-
- Let the dough rest for 10 minutes.
- In a saucepan, heat the ghee.

Put the batter in a saucepan.

Make sure to brown all sides of the pancakes.

Spicy Sausage Scramble
Ingredients:

- Whole powdered egg 4 tbsp.
- Freeze-dried sausage 4 tbsp.
- Dried tomatoes 6
- Tomato-sauce powder 1 tbsp.
- 1/2 teaspoon dried herb (oregano).
-
-
Ghee 1 tbsp.

Frozen-dried Parmesan cheese 2 tbsp.

-
-

Instructions:

- In a medium-sized zip-lock container, combine the dried eggs, dried tomatoes, sausage scraps, dried herb, and tomato sauce.
- Set aside the rest of the ingredients.
- Mix the Sausage Scramble mixture with half a cup of water.
- Mix well and compare.
- In a saucepan, heat the ghee under low pressure.
-

Mix the egg mixture and allow to stand for 30 seconds.

Before the eggs are tender, ramble gently.

Turn off the heat and use Parmesan to brush your hair

.

<u>Steamed Spinach Omelet</u>
Instructions:

- Dried egg 4 tbsp.
- Spinach powder 1 tsp.
- Salt
- Pepper
- Freeze-dried Parmesan cheese 1 tbsp.

Instructions:

- In a medium-sized zip lock bag, mix the powdered eggs and spinach powder.
- For the Steamed Spinach omelet mix, attach 1/3 cup of water to the container.
- Adjust well to compare and blend.
- Place the mixture in a bag. Cover it and let it sit for 5-10 minutes.
- To simmer, add 2 cups water to a saucepan.
- Place the zip lock inside the pot.
- Turn down the heat and then cover with a blanket.

Allow the eggs to steam roast for about 10 minutes or until the top is browned.

Very Berry Smoothie Ingredients:
   Frozen mixed berries 1 cup

- Banana 1
- 2 tbsp. Wheat berries, rolled oats (gluten free) Orange
- juice 1/3 cup

-
-

Instructions:

- Mix all products in a processor.
- You can run a fast cycle until it becomes frothy.
-

Layer the parchment or nonstick paper over the dehydrator tray.

- Dry for 6-12 hours at 115F/46C, until thoroughly dried and hard.
- Allow the air to cool to room temperature.
-
-
-
- In a grinder, grind the smoothie mixture into a fine powder.
- Place in a small sealed bag.

Place the smoothie mixture in a large container or saucepan.

Mix well, then add 1/3 cup of water.

Allow to rehydrate for five to ten minutes. Mix again and let it sit for a few minutes.

Sweet Potato Bark
Ingredients:

- Approx. 13 ounces before peeling one large Sweet Potatoes
- Apple Juice ½ cup Real Maple Syrup 1 tbsp. Cinnamon 1
- tsp.

Instructions:

- Peel the sweet potatoes, and then break them into bits.
- Boil, rinse, and blend until smooth.

- Mix in the apple juice, cinnamon, maple syrup. If you prefer nutmeg, substitute half the cinnamon.

- Blend the mashed sweet potatoes until velvety, through a mixer. If the mixer is struggling with the combination, add a couple more spoons of juice or water.
- Protect dehydration trays with non-stick sheets, parchment paper, or patches of fruit leather provided with your dehydrator.
- Placed on sealed dehydrator trays, finely and as uniformly as possible. The thickness of the eighth in.

- Dehydrate for 8 to 10 hours at 135 ° C.
- After about six hours of drying, peel off the nonstick layers. Then, turn the skin over to expose the lower portion to heated air. You can place the bark directly onto the mesh dehydrate trays without the use of non-stick mats.

- The sweet potato sheet either tears like fruit leather or breaks into the bark, based on how long you dehydrate it. You can choose to dry it onto the leather phase for snacking and short-term use.
- One big or two medium sweet potatoes (about 13 ounces before peeling) generate nearly 3/4 cup of bark and measure 21/2 ounces. For bigger batches, increasing the products equitably.

Chapter 4: Lunch and Dinner Meal Recipes Using Dehydrated Foods

You can use dehydrated fruits and veggies for breakfast and lunch in a wide variety of main dishes. They not only enhance the flavor of the recipe, but also make it fast and easy to prepare.

Let's take a look at some quick and easy dinner and lunch recipes using dehydrated foods.

4.1 Lunch Recipes

Backcountry   Feijoada
Ingredients:

- Dehydrated rice 1/4 cup (cooked)
- Dehydrated black-beans 1/4 cup
- Dehydrated ground beef 2 tbsps.
- 30g/1oz beef jerky one pack Dehydrated
- ham 1 tbsp.
- 1 tsp. Roast beef mixture gravy.
- Dried parsley 1 tsp.
- Bouillon powder 1/2 tsp.
- Sweet smoked paprika 1/2 tsp.
-
-
   1/4 tsp. onion powder Garlic
   powder 1/8 teaspoon.

Instructions:

- Spoon the mixture Feijoada and a cup of water into the skillet.
- Bring to a boil on a medium flame.
-
- Cook for about 10 minutes, stirring occasionally.

Cover the pan and let it cool for five minutes.

Bulgur Chili Ingredients:

- Olive oil 1 tsp.
- Red onion chopped, 1/2
-
- Red bell pepper chopped, 1/2
- 1/2 cup canned tomatoes

Instant-cooking Bulgur 1/4 Cup
Mexican seasoning 1 Tsp Salt and
pepper

- Kidney beans canned, 1/4 cup (drained)
- 70% cacao dark chocolate 10 grams

Instructions:

- Over moderate flame heat olive oil in a skillet. Add sliced onions, and simmer until tender.
- Mix in seasonings of peppers, Mexican, and Bulgur.
- Cook the mixture for about a minute on medium heat to activate the flavor.

- Spill in 1/2 cup water and tomatoes; mix and simmer gently.
- Add salt and pepper.
- Boil the kidney beans until almost all of the water has been drained.

- Switch from heat and refrigerate to room temperature.
- Place the bulgur chili mixture on a parchment-lined tray or nonstick layer.

- Dehydrate for 8-10 hours at 52C/125F, until stiff.
- The Dry Meal can be stored in a ziplock bag.
-

Add the dry mixture of bulgur chili to the pan. Mix well with a cup water.

- Continue cooking over medium heat and let it boil.
- Cook for approximately 5 minutes, stirring frequently.
-
- Turn off the heat.

Cover the food with a lid and allow it to sit for five more minutes.

- Add the chunks of chocolate and enjoy it!

Chickpea and Spinach Curry
Ingredients:
- Dehydrated basmati rice 1/4 cup (cooked)
- Garbanzo beans canned-chickpeas dehydrated 1/4 cup Coconut
- milk powder 2 Tbsps.

- Spinach powder 1 tbsps. Or a handful dehydrated spinach

- Curry powder 1/2 tsp. (mild)
- Salt, to taste

Instructions:

- Add the curry mixture of spinach and chickpea into a pot, then add 1 cup of water.
- Stirring occasionally and let it cook until it has rehydrated, bringing to a boil for about 10 minutes.

Curried Pumpkin Soup

Ingredients:
- Curried-pumpkin powder 1/4 cup
- Coconut-milk powder 3 tbsps.
- Salt and pepper Pumpkin seeds 1
- tsp.

Instructions:

- Add the dry mix of curry with a cup of water into the skillet.
- Mix well.
- Place the pot on a medium flame and stir it occasionally. Then let it boil.
- Salt and pepper to taste.

Reduce the heat and add pumpkin seeds to the soup.

Curried Zucchini Soup

Ingredients:

- Dehydrated zucchini-powder 4 tbsp.
- Coconut-milk powder 2 Tbsp.
-
- Dehydrated mild curry-powder 1 tsp (optional). Croutons one handful

Instructions:

- Take a medium-sized sealable plastic freezer bag, mix the coconut milk powder, zucchini powder, and dehydrated curry-paste.
- Spill the soup blend into a saucepan.
- Add 1 cup of hot water slowly and stir.
-
- Allow it to sit for five minutes to fully hydrate. Serve with croutons.

Chickpea and vegetable curry ingredients:

- Coconut-oil 1 tbsps.
- Diced red onions, 1 Garam-masala
- Powder 2 tsp.
- Turmeric powder 1 tsp.
- Chili powder 1/2 tsp.
- Mixture of vegetables chopped (one large sweet potato, one carrot, and green beans) 1.5kg/3.3lb

- 400g/14oz drained chickpeas; one can
- Salt to taste
- One handful of coriander leaves, chopped Coconut-
- milk Powder 8 tbsps.

Instructions:

- In any large saucepan, heat the olive oil.
- Continue to cook the onions until softened and golden brown. Mix in the
- spices and heat for one minute.
-

Add the vegetables and 1 cup water. Bring to a boil, then add the seasoning. Reduce heat to medium-low.

- Keep a cover on and allow simmering for around 30-40 minutes, until vegetables are tender.
  Mix in chickpea leaves and coriander. Combine well. Continue to boil for a few minutes. Reduce the heat to a low setting and let it cool completely.

  Place the chickpea and vegetable curry mixture on parchment or nonstick paper sheets.

- Dehydrate for 8-10 hours at 63C/145F, until crispy. Split the dried food into four equal proportions (approximately 100 gr/3.5 oz. apiece) and place it in different zip-lock pouches. Add two tbsps. Of coconut milk powder to each bag and lock the bag with a seal.
- To rehydrate a single serving:
-    Place the dried food in a saucepan and apply 2/3 to 1 cup of water.
- Put to simmer, and continue to cook until rehydrated, stirring regularly for around 10-15 minutes. Offer with Chapatti or Tortilla.

Moussaka Casserole
Ingredients:

- Parchment paper
- Eggplant 1 medium
- 1 Green bell pepper
- Red bell pepper 1
- Tomato 1
- Olive oil 2 Tbsps. (1 tbsp). For drizzling, use two tablespoons. For frying

- Diced onion, 1
- 2 finely chopped garlic cloves

500g lean beef mince
Canned tomatoes 1 Cup (crushed).
Salt and Pepper
Sugar
1 teaspoon dried parsley Fresh chopped parsley 1 tsp.

Instructions:

Heat the oven to 400°F/200C. Sprinkle parchment on a baking sheet.

paper.
- Chop peppers, eggplant, and tomatoes roughly.
- Add vegetables to a baking dish. Sprinkle with salt, then glaze with olive oil.

- Cook vegetables until soft, for around 20-30 minutes.
- In a large frying pan, heat the oil. Add the garlic and onion. Stirring constantly, cook the onions until they are softened and light brown.

- Stir in the ground beef and continue to cook until completely brown. Move-in a colander. Wash and drain.
- In the frying pan, transfer the meat back. Spill the diced tomatoes into a frying pan along with the juice. Switch to low heat.
- Add parsley and roasted vegetables, and mix well. Sprinkle with salt, sugar, and pepper, according to taste. Keep a cover on, and keep for another 5 minutes to cook.
- Please turn off the flame. Allow it to cool completely. Pour moussaka on non-stick plates or parchment paper-lined dehydrator trays.
- Dehydrate for 8-10 hours at 63C/145F, until crispy.
- Divide the moussaka into small pieces and place them in zip-lock bags.
- Mix the dry moussaka with 1 cup water in a skillet.

- Put the pan and bring to a simmer over moderate heat—Fry for about 5 minutes, stirring frequently.
- Turn down the heat, cover, and let another 5-10 minutes stand to rehydrate food entirely.

-

- Easy Cheesy Salmon
- Pasta Ingredients:
-

- Full cream powdered milk 1 tbsps.
- 2 tbsps freeze-dried powdered cheese cheddar cheese.
  All-purpose flour 1 tsp.
  Pre-cooked and dehydrated pasta 1/3 cup

  Salt, to taste
  Ghee 1 tbsps.
  One pouch of smoked salmon (around 70g/2.5 oz.

Instructions:

- Add pasta and 1/3 cup of water into a saucepan.
- Bring to a boil, then add the seasonings.
-

Reduce heat to medium and continue to stir for approximately 5 minutes or until rehydrated.

- Take the saucepan off the flame.
- Add the powdered milk and cheese sauce from your pouch. Blend in the
- ghee until smooth. Enjoy salmon flakes with your favorite garnish   and serve!

Georgian Chicken Stew
Ingredients:
-

- Olive oil 1 tbsps.
- 2 Lb. 2 Lb.
-
- Sliced red onion, 2
- Red bell pepper strips thin 2
-
- Thin strips of sliced green bell pepper 2
-

400g/ 14 oz. One can of diced tomatoes

Chicken stock 1 cup

Salt, to taste

   1 tbsps. khmeli-suneli, traditional Georgian spice mix. The spices and herbs used in khmeli suneli are dills, coriander, bay leaf, fenugreek, marjoram, black pepper, parsley, thyme, celery, mind, and hyssop). If this blend is not found in your area, replace it with the chicken spice of your choice. Cooked rice 2 cups

   Instructions: Finely chopped fresh herbs (1 cup) (flat parsley:

- In a large frying pan, add oil and turn the heat on.
- Cook the meat until it turns golden brown. Mix in the chopped onion.

Continue cooking for 5 minutes, stirring occasionally.

- Add tomatoes, bell peppers, and stock of chicken.
- Bring the salt, Khmeli Suneli and water to a boil. Season with salt to taste.

- Cover and simmer, on low heat and leave for another 15-20 minutes to fry.
- Add the chopped herbs and cooked rice. Mix well and sauté together for a few minutes.
- Take off the heat and adequately let cool.
- Place the chicken stew on parchment paper-covered baking sheets.

- Dehydrate for 4-8 hours at 63C/145F, until hard.
- Divide the dried food into equal portions (approximately 1 Cup per piece) and place it in different ziplock containers.

- Place the dried food in a skillet and pour 1 cup of water.
- Boil the mixture and let it cook for about 10-15 minutes stirring occasionally or until it is rehydrated.

Mac N Cheese Recipes that are Good and Old:

- Full cream powdered milk 1 tbsps.
- Three tablespoons of freeze-dried powdered cheddar cheese.
- All-purpose flour 1 tsp.

- Pre-cooked and dehydrated pasta 1/3 cup

Salt, to taste
Ghee 1 tbsps.

Instructions:

-
-
-
-

Combine the powdered milk, flour and cheese in a sealed bag.

Put 1/3 cup water and pasta in a saucepan.
Let it simmer, and then add the seasonings to suit your taste.

Reduce the heat to normal, mix frequently, cook for approximately 5 minutes, then rehydrate.

- Let the heat turned off.
- Add the powdered cheese sauce and milk from the packet. Mix
- in the ghee and stir until it is well incorporated.

Ground Turkey Taco Stew
Ingredients:

- Chopped red onion, 1
- 1 kg or 22.2 lb lean turkey mince
- 2 chopped red bell peppers
- 400g/14oz drained black beans, 1 can
- 340g/12oz drained sweet corn, 1 can
- Organic 1 packet Santa Maria taco spice mix
-
-

400g/14oz diced tomato 1 can

Salt, according to taste
Fresh cilantro or coriander leaves chopped, 1 bunch Freeze dried
powdered cheddar cheese 1 Tbsp.
One handful of tortilla chips or corn chips crumbled

Instructions:
- Take a normal sized pan, and heat olive oil.
- In the same skillet, toss in the onion and cook until soft and golden. Roast
- the meat in the skillet until it is fully cooked. Transfer the meat to a colander.

- Strain the water, and transfer to the skillet.
- You can also add a mix of sweet corn, red peppers, beans, and taco seasoning.

   Cook for about 5 minutes, stirring occasionally. Mix the chopped tomatoes with their juice and add to the bowl. Stir and combine.

   To season and taste, add chopped cilantro.

-

- Reduce the heat to a simmer, cover with a lid and steam for 15 more
  minutes.

- Take off entirely from the heat, and let it cool.
- Place the Ground Turkey Taco Stew onto parchment paper-lined or nonstick dehydrator trays.

- Dehydrate for 8-12 hours at 63C/145F, until crispy.
- Let the temperature fall to cool.
-

Divide the dried meal into equal portions (approximately 1 c each) and place it in different ziplock containers.

- To rehydrate 1 serving:
- In a large pot, combine the dry ground Turkey Taco Stew with 1 cup water.

- Over medium heat, place the pot and let it boil.
- Cook for 5 minutes, stirring every now and again.
-

Turn off the heat and cover the pan. Let the food rest for 6-10 minutes to fully rehydrate.

- Sprinkle with crushed corn chips and mix in cheese powder to serve.

Honolulu Curry
Ingredients:

- Dehydrated pre-cooked basmati rice 1/3 cup Dehydrated
- shrimp 2 tbsps.
- Dehydrated canned-pineapples 2 tbsps.
- Mild curry powder 1 teaspoon.
- Coconut-milk powder 2 teaspoons.

Instructions:

- Combine all the ingredients in a sealed plastic container that is medium to large.
  Put 1 cup of water and dry curry into the pot.
  Place the pot on medium heat and allow it to boil.
  Cook for approximately 10 minutes, stirring every now and again.

- Let it rest without heat, closed for the next 5 minutes to rehydrate the dish properly.

Hot   Borscht
Ingredients:

- Dehydrated shredded pickled beetroots 2 tbsp.
- Dehydrated or freeze-dried beef 2 tbsp 1 tbsp.
- Beetroot powder (Organic preferred) Quick-cook
- mashed potatoes 1 Tbsp.
- Onion powder 1 tsp.
- Vegetable bouillon powder 1/4

Salt, according to taste
Pepper, according to taste

Instructions:

- Blend the supplies in a zip lock container.
- Mix the Hot Borscht mix with 1 cup water in a large pot.

- Over medium heat, place the pot and let it boil.
- Cook for 5 minutes, stirring every now and again.

Reduce the heat and cover the pan with a lid. Let the food rest for 5 minutes to fully rehydrate.

Lazy Golubtsi Ingredients:
Olive oil 1 tbsp.
Lean beef-mince 400 grams
Cooked rice 2/3 cup of riced cauliflower 1 cup
- Shredded cabbage 2 cups Tomato paste 1 tbsp.
Beef stock 2/3 cup

-
-
-
- Salt and pepper
- Onion, 1 small

Instructions:

- In a skillet, heat olive oil over a moderate flame. Fry the onion frequently, stirring softly.
- Stir in the ground beef and fry until cooked thoroughly.
- Add riced cauliflower. Mix together for 5 minutes.
-

Mix beef stock with shredded cabbage and tomato paste. Season to taste.

- Lower the flame speed to low, place on a top, and cook for about 15-20 minutes until the cabbage is tender.
- Remove altogether from the heat, and let it completely cool.
- Place the Lazy Golubtsi mix on parchment or non-stick paper lined dehydrator trays.

- Dehydrate for 10-12 hours at 63 ° C (145 ° F), until dried completely and crumbly.
- Split the Lazy Golubtsi mixture divided into two equal proportions and packed into different zip-lock pouches.
- Pour the dried Golubtsi Lazy combination and 1 cup of water into a pot.
- Put to a boil and simmer until it has rehydrated, stirring regularly for around 10 minutes.
- Miso Mushroom Soup
- Ingredients:

- Dried and powdered shiitake mushrooms, 2 medium Vegetable
- bouillon powder 1 tsp.
- 1 packet instant miso soup 1 tsp. Dried wakame seaweeds 1
- teaspoon.

Instructions:

- Put the products together in a plastic zip-lock container.
- Mix the Miso Mushroom Soup in a cup.
-
- Mix 1 cup hot water with the mixture.

Cover with a cloth and let sit for five minutes.

Tomato Basil Soup
Ingredients:
- Powdered tomato sauce 2 tsp.
- Powdered vegetable broth 1 tsp. Dried
- basil 1/2 teaspoon.

Instructions:

- Put the products together in a plastic zip-lock container. Pour the water into a cup with tomato basil broth.
- Stir in 1 cup of hot water.
- Mix well, cover with a lid and let sit for five minutes.

-

- Tomato Seafood
- Chowder Ingredients:
- Powdered tomato sauce powder 2 tbsp.
- Cubes of vegetable bouillon 1/4
  Fish seasoning 1 tsp.
  Dehydrated shrimp 1 tbsp.
- Dehydrated canned mussel 1 tbsp.
  Imitation crab meat 1 Tbsp.

  Salt and pepper

Instructions:

- In a mid-sized zip lock case, combine all the ingredients, excluding salt and pepper. In the pot, pour dry soup mixture with 1 and 1/4 cup water, and mix equally.
- Over medium heat, place the pot and let it boil. Add the seasoning according to the taste.
- Lower the heat temperature to low, and cook for about 5 minutes, stirring occasionally.
- Turn the flame down, cover with a lid, and let sit to rehydrate meal for another 5-10 minutes fully.

Tsampa Mushroom Soup
Ingredients:
- Traditional Tsampa Cereal 2 tbsp.
- Porcini mushrooms, approximately 10g dried 1 handful.
- Dehydrated canned-lentils, 1 tbsp.
-
- 1 tsp powdered vegetable bouillon.
-

Dried parsley 1 tsp.
- 1 tbsp.

Instructions:

- Add all of the ingredients in a zip-lock pouch of medium size. Load dry mixture of soup and 1 cup of water into the pot, and mix properly.
- Let them soak for five minutes.
- Place the pot on medium heat and allow it to boil. Stir occasionally for 5 minutes.

    Remove the pot from the heat and cover it with a lid. Let the pot stand for 8-10 minutes to completely rehydrate the food.

Unstuffed Peppers

Ingredients:
- Olive oil 1 tsp.
- Chopped small onion, 1
- 1 clove garlic, minced
- 5.30oz lean beef mince 150g
- Chopped green bell pepper 1
- 1 cup sliced canned tomatoes
- Salt and sugar
- Pinch of dried basil
- Pinch of dried oregano

- Cooked rice 1/2 cup
-

- Instructions:
-
  - Take a large skillet and add oil and let it heat. Add the chopped garlic and onions, and fry until crispy and fluffy.
- Stir in the ground beef and cook unless cooked thoroughly. Move-in a colander. Strain. Place meat back into the skillet.
- Top in green pepper and keep cooking for about 5 minutes.
- Mix the juice and the chopped tomatoes in a skillet. Salt and sugar can
- be added to the mixture according to your taste. To taste, add dried basil and oregano.

- Turn the heating off. Put a cover on, and wait for 10 minutes to cook.
- Mix in the rice and boil for about 5 minutes.
-
- Take the heat off completely and allow it to cool.

Place the unstuffed peppers on a dehydrator tray covered with nonstick parchment or a layer of parchment.

    Allow to dry at 63C/145F for 8-10 hours, or until firm.
    Place dry food in a zipper-lock container.
    Add the beef and pepper to the saucepan. Pour 1 cup water. Mix well.

    Place the pot on medium heat and allow it to boil.

    Cook for another 5 minutes, stirring every now and again.

- Lower the temperature of the heat and put on a lid, and allow to rest for another 8-10 minutes to rehydrate food fully.

Vegetable Yellow Curry

Ingredients:

- 3.53 oz. basmati rice 100 grams Thai
- yellow curry paste 1 tbsp. Frozen
- vegetable mix 2 cups Coconut milk
- powder 4 tbsp.

Instructions:

- Cook the packaged rice as per directions on the box.
- Drain it and allow it to cool.
-

Layer vegetables, beans, and curry paste on nonstick or parchment paper lined trays.

- Dry for 4-8 hours, at 135F/57C.
- Place the dehydrated food into a zip-lock bag. Seal the bag with powdered coconut milk.

- Stir curry vegetables with 2 cups of water into the pot.
- Bring the pot to a boil on a medium heat flame.
-
- Allow to simmer for 5 minutes, stirring occasionally.

Reduce the heat and cover the container with a lid. Allow food to rest for 5-10 minutes more. Backcountry Thanksgiving Ingredients:

- 30 g stuffing mix (about ½ c)

- 25 g quick-cook potatoes (about 1/4 c)
-
  Turkey jerky30 g
- 35 g dried cranberries (about ¼ c)   Celery
- seed ⅛ tsp. Or celery flakes1 tbsp.
- Gravy powder2 tsp.
- Oil or butter

Instructions:

- Boil around 1 3/4 cup of water, and switch off the burner.
- Mix the mixture into the skillet and stir well. All the ingredients will be covered by the water.

- Close the lid of your pot and place it in a cozy (or cloth hat) position.
- Wait approximately 15 minutes to make sure everything gets extensively rehydrated (without peaking).
- Then, confirm to see if it requires a little more water or time.
- Mix it all together and add some butter or oil to help add the dehydrated fat back in.

Ingredients for Rugged Mountain Glory Bacon & Grits:

- About 56 g Instant grits 2 packets
- Half small bag of real bacon bits or dehydrated Ham
- Parmesan cheese 1 Tbsp. Parmesan cheese 1 Tbsp.
-

Instructions:

- Boil around 1 1/4 cups of water, and then switch off your burner.   Add
- all to the pot, and mix to blend. The water will cover all the mixes.
  Place the bowl in a safe place.

  Allow everything to hydrate for around 10 to 15 minutes.
  Next, check to see if the plant needs more water or extra time.
  Mix everything together and then add a bit of butter or oil, and
  sriracha, if needed. Enjoy it!

Beef Noodle Soup
Ingredients:
- Powdered beef, vegetable, or chicken bouillon 1 tsp
- 1/4 cup dried vegetable mix
-
- About 50g Ramen noodles in 1 block
Natural low sodium jerky, 25 g

Instructions:

- Boil about 3 cups of water, then switch off your burner.
- Mix both ingredients in a bowl.
-
- Cover the bowl with the lid and place it in a safe spot.
-
- Wait around 10-15 minutes to see to it that everything is adequately rehydrated.
- Then, verify to see if it requires a little more water or time. For
- a soup-like quality, there will be a bit of extra oil.
- Mix well and, if necessary, add a little butter or oil to the mixture.

4.2 Dinner Recipes
Beef & Barley Stew
Ingredients:

- Dehydrated cooked-barley 1/3 cup
- Dehydrated-ground beef 1/4 cup
- Dehydrated carrots 1 tbsp.
- Dehydrated-green beans 1 tbsp.
- Dehydrated celery 1 tsp.
- 1 tbsp powdered tomato sauce.
- Dried thyme 1 tsp.
- Powdered low-sodium Bouillon 1 tsp.

Instructions:

- Load the Beef & Barley Stew mixture and add 1 cup sugar into the pot.
- Place the pot on a medium flame and allow it to boil.
-
- Cook for approximately 10 minutes, stirring frequently.

Remove from heat and cover with a lid. Let the food sit for 10 minutes to completely rehydrate.

Beef Alfredo
Ingredients
- Dehydrated and pre-cooked pasta3/4 cup Beef
- mince (freeze-dried) 1/2 cup
- Cheddar cheese (freeze-dried) 2 tbsps.
- Powdered mozzarella cheese (freeze-dried) 1 tbsp.
- 1 tbsp powdered full-cream milk.
- All-purpose flour 1 tsp.
- 1 tsp. Garlic powder
- Salt and pepper Ghee 1 teaspoon.

Instructions:

- In a middle-sized sealed bag, combine pasta and freeze-dried beef. In
- another container, add the cheese, powdered milk, flour, and garlic powder.
- Load the Beef Alfredo mix into a pot.
- Mix 3/4 cup of water into the mixture and allow to sit for five minutes.
- Bring it to boil, then add the seasonings according to your preference.
Reduce heat to a minimum and cook frequently, stirring until rehydrated.
- Remove the pot from oil, and whisk in the mixture of ghee and cheese sauce.
- Note: You can use regular, non-dehydrated pasta to create this recipe too. Cook them in salted, boiling pots as indicated on the packet. Strain the water with around 2/3 cup left, then whisk in the mix of sauce and ghee.

Easy Chili Mac Ingredients:

- Dehydrated and pre-cooked pasta 2/3 cup
- 1/4 cup dehydrated ground meat (beef)
- Powdered tomato sauce 2 Tbsps.
-
- Chili powder one pinch
- 1 handful grated cheddar or parmesan cheese

Ingredients:

- In a medium-sized sealable plastic bag, add dried ground beef, rice, dried beans, chili, and powdered tomato sauce.

- Pour the mixture of chili mac into a bowl.
- Mix the water in a cup. Bring to boil and adjust seasonings to taste.

- Lower the heat to a minimum, and cook periodically, stirring for around 10 minutes, or until rehydrated.
- Take the pot down from the heat, and pour in the cheese.

Irish Stew
Ingredients
- Freeze-dried chopped potatoes or dehydrated potatoes 1/4 cup
- Freeze-dried beef chunks or dried, canned beef 1/4 cup
- Dehydrated carrots 2 tsp.
- Dehydrated green beans 1 tablespoon.
- 1 tbsp. Dried fried onions (or freeze-dried red onions (caramelized).
-
- Powdered beef gravy 1 Tbsp.
- Dried thyme 1 tsp.
Powdered low-sodium Bouillon 1 tsp.

Instructions:

- Combine all the products in a sealable plastic container of medium lengths.
- Put Irish Stew mixture and 1/4 cup of water into a saucepan; Over
- medium heat, place the pot, and let it boil.
- Remove from heat and cover with a lid. Allow to cool completely for about 15 to 20 minutes.

- You can make this dish genuinely Irish by removing 1/4 cup of water from the recipe and replacing it with dark Guinness beer.

- Italian Stew

Ingredients:
- Dried grilled vegetables 1/4 cup
- 1/2 cup minced frozen meat (beef) Powdered
- tomato sauce 1 Tbsp.
- Dried oregano 1/4 tsp.
  Dried basil 1/4 tsp.
- Parmesan cheese (freeze-dried and grated) 2 tbsps. Ghee
- 1 tbsp.

Instructions:

- To make Italian Stew combine all the dried ingredients in a sealed bag of medium scale. Spoon the mixture of the Italian stew into the frying pan and pour 3/4 cup hot water.
- Over medium flame, place the pan and let it boil.
- Cook for about 10 minutes, stirring frequently.
-

  Takedown from the flame, covering with a lid and let stay to rehydrate meal for another five minutes fully. Stir in Parmesan cheese and ghee.

Kale Mac and Kale Cheese
Ingredients:
- Powdered full cream milk 1 tbsp.
- 2 tbsps.
-
- Kale powder 1 tbsp.
- Pre-cooked and dehydrated pasta shells 1 1/2
- Salt, depending on taste Ghee 1 Tbsp.

Instructions:

- In a plastic sealable container, combine the powdered milk, kale powder, and cheese. Pour the pasta into a saucepan with 1 cup of water. Take
- to a simmer, and sample the season.
- Reduce the heat to medium and continue cooking, stirring occasionally, for approximately 5-10 minutes or until the mixture is rehydrated.

- Let the heat off the pot.
- Add milk and cheese to the container.

- Blend the ghee until it is melted.

Moroccan Stew
Ingredients:
- Beef mince (freeze-dried) 1/2 cup
- Chickpeas dehydrated (canned), 2 tbsps.
- 1 tbsp. dehydrated lentils.
- Caramelized red onions (freeze-dried), 1 tbsp.
- 1 tbsp powdered tomato sauce.
- Dehydrated and cooked rice 1 tbsp Moroccan seasoning 1 teaspoon.

Instructions:
- Combine all of the above-mentioned ingredients in a medium shaped sealed bag for Moroccan Stew.
- Spoon the mixture of the Moroccan Stew into the pot with 1 cup of water.
- Over medium flame, place the pot and let it boil.
- Boil for approximately 10 minutes, stirring frequently.
-

Cover the pan with a lid and remove from the flame. Let it sit to rehydrate for five more minutes.

Muja Dara: Lebanese Lentil Stew
Ingredients:

- Dehydrated and cooked rice 1/2 cup
- Dehydrated and canned lentils 1/4 cup Crispy
- fried onions 2 tbsps.
- Powdered low-sodium Bouillon 1 tsp.
- Ground cumin 1/4 tsp.
  Ground coriander 1/4 tsp.
  Salt, according to taste.

Instructions:

- Mix all the products in a sealable plastic container of medium lengths.
- Mix the ingredients in a saucepan. Add 1 cup water.
-

Bring it to a boil, then simmer for approximately 10 minutes, or until the vegetables are tender.

Mushroom Mac N Cheese
Ingredients:

- Dehydrated and pre-cooked pasta2/3 cup
- Dried porcini mushrooms 1 handful Dried
- thyme 1/2 tsp.
- 1 tbsp powdered full-cream milk.
- Powdered cheddar cheese (freeze-dried) 3
- tbsps. All-purpose flour 1 tsp. Salt according to
- taste Ghee 1 teaspoon.
-

Instructions:

- In a medium-sized sealable plastic container, mix the pasta, thyme, and mushrooms.
- In another container, combine the powdered milk, cheese, and flour.
- Pour the Mushroom Mac mixture into a bowl. Stir well in 1/3 cup water, then let sit for 5 minutes.
- Take to a simmer, and add the season according to your taste. Lower the
- heat to a minimum, and frequently cook, stirring until rehydrated. Take the pot from heat and whisk in cheese sauce and ghee.

Mushroom Stroganoff

Ingredients:
- Powdered full cream milk 1 tbsp.
- All-purpose flour 1 tsp.
- Thyme 1/2 tsp.
- Dried mushrooms 2 Tbsps. Ghee
- 1 tablespoon.
- Small shallot 1
- Salt and pepper

Instructions:

- In a medium-sized sealable freezer bag, combine the powdered milk, thyme, rice, and mushrooms.
- Add half cup of water to the bag; mix well and let stay for 10 minutes.
- While the mushroom is resting, take a frying pan, heat ghee, add the chopped onions and fry until tender.
- Add mushrooms to the pan along with liquid they have been soaking in.
- Take to a simmer, and stir regularly—top with salt and pepper, to taste.

Lower the heat to a minimum, and boil until cooked down, stirring for around 2 minutes.
- Serve stroganoff with the mushroom over mashed potatoes, pasta, or rice.

Pasta Marinara

Ingredients:
- Dehydrated and cooked pasta (2.82oz) 80 grams Dehydrated
- canned mussel 2 tbsps.
- Dehydrated shrimp 1 tbsp.

- Powdered tomato sauce 2 tbsps.
- Dried basil 1pinch
- Dry oregano 1 pinch Instructions:

- Blend the supplies in a zip-lock container.
- Add the marinara pasta mix to the bowl.
-
- Place the pot in a saucepan and heat on medium heat.
-

Cook for 10 minutes, stirring frequently.

Reduce the heat to a low setting, cover the container with a lid and let it sit for 5 minutes more to fully rehydrate the food.

Penne Puttanesca
Ingredients:
- Whole-wheat penne pasta4 cups Olive
- oil 1 tbsp.
- Minced garlic cloves, 3
-
- Diced red onion,1
- Anchovy fillets 6
- 1 can diced tomatoes 2 tbsps.
-
- Kalamata olives, chopped and pitted1/4 cup Arrabbiata
- Seasoning 1 tsp.
- Salt and sugar
2 tbsps fresh and finely chopped flat leaf parsley.
Parmesan cheese (freeze dried and grated) 4 Tbsps.

Instructions:

- Boil pasta in boiling salted water, as instructed by the box.
- Put the pasta in ice water to wash. Drain the pasta and set aside.
-

In a saucepan, heat olive oil under low pressure. For 3 minutes, cook the garlic and onion gently, stirring often. Stir in the anchovies and fry until they are cooked.

- Decrease heat to a minimum, put a cap on, and leave for ten minutes to boil before the sauce is thickened moderately. Clear entirely from the heat, and let it cool.
- Place pasta and sauce, lined with non-stick sheets or parchment paper, on different dehydrator plates.
- Dehydrate for 2–4 hours at 57 ° C (134 ° F) before the paste has dried. Then remove the pasta plates from the dehydrator and dehydrate the sauce for another 4–8 hours, before it is stiff and rigid.
- Split the dehydrated sauce and pasta into four equal sections, and put them into different zip lock containers.
- Place the dried food in a saucepan and pour 1 cup of water.
- Bring to a boil, and let it simmer for 10 minutes. Stir frequently.

- Serve finished with Parmesan sliced cheese.

Pumpkin Curry with Spinach, Chickpeas and Other
Ingredients:

- Dehydrated and cooked basmati rice 1/4 cup
- Can and dehydrated chickpeas 1/4 Cup Dehydrated
- spinach 2 tablespoons
-
- 2 tbsp powdered curried pumpkin.
- 2 tbsp powdered coconut milk Salt

Instructions:

- Combine the supplies in a zip lock container. Spill dehydrated curry mix into the bowl; mix well and add 1/2 to 2/3 cup of water.
- Put the pot and bring to a simmer over medium flame.
- Seasons can be added to suit your personal taste.
-
- Cook for about 10 minutes, stirring frequently.

Cover the pan with a lid and let it cool for 5 minutes.

Before serving.

Pumpkin Gnocchi
Ingredients:

- Pumpkin powder 2 tbsps.
- 1 tbsp whole egg powder.
- All-purpose flour 4 tbsps.
- Salt according to taste Ghee
- 1 tablespoon.
- Dried sage 1/2 tsp.
- Parmesan cheese (freeze dried and grated) 1 Tbsp.

Instructions:

- Blend all dumpling ingredients in a sealable bag. Gradually introduce the pumpkin gnocchi mixture with 1/4 cup of water, 1 tbsp. at the moment.

- Knead soft dough, which slightly sticks.
- Make 2 3/4-inch "sausages" from the dough (2 cm).
- Reduce rising one into 3/4 inch (2 cm), long "pillows."

Bring 2 cups of water to a boil in a saucepan. Add a little salt.
-

The gnocchi is then cooked, and the dumplings are moved upwards.

   Drain the dumplings
- Place the gnocchi pot back to heat.
- Stir in the sage and ghee. Cook for about 1 minute, stirring occasionally.
-
- Get out of the heat.

Enjoy the Parmesan gnocchi and toss it with.

Ingredients for Quinoa and
Crab Curry:

- Cooked dehydrated quinoa1/4 cup
- 1/4 cup imitation dehydrated crab meat (gluten free)
-

Dehydrated powdered mild curry or yellow Thai curry paste or 1 tsp
   Powdered coconut milk 2 tbsps.

Instructions:

- Combine all the products in a sealable plastic container of medium lengths. Pour a mix of quinoa and crab curry into the skillet and pour 1 cup of water.

- Put the pot and bring to the boil over moderate heat.
- Cook for 5 minutes, stirring frequently.
-

Cover the pan with a lid and remove from heat. Let cool for 5 minutes.

Ingredients for Quinoa, Lentil, and Kale Stew:

- Dehydrated and cooked quinoa1/4 cup
- Dehydrated Beluga lentils and cooked black lentils 1/4 Cup Powdered
- coconut milk 2 Tbsps.
- Powdered kale 1 tsp.
- Powdered mild curry 1 teaspoon.
- Cube of vegetable Bouillon 1/4
-

    Caramelized red onion (freeze dried) - 10g /0.35oz 1 tablespoon Salt

Instructions:

- Mix all of the products in a zip lock container.
- Put the stew mix of quinoa and kale in a bowl. Add 1 cup of water.

- Take to a boil and simmer until it has rehydrated, stirring regularly for around 10 minutes.

Roasted Ratatouille
Ingredients:

- Roughly chopped eggplant, 1 medium
- Zucchini, diced 2 small
- 1 diced red bell pepper, 1
- diced yellow bell pepper, 1
- olive oil 1 tbsp.
- Finely chopped red onions, 1
-
-
- Minced garlic cloves, 2 diced
- tomatoes 1 can Herbs de
- Provence 1 tbsp.

Salt and Pepper

Instructions:

- Let the oven temperature rise to 200C/400F. Place rimmed parchment paper to the baking plate.
- On a prepared baking tray, put the zucchini, eggplant, and peppers. Bake until tender, for almost 30 minutes.
- In a casserole dish, heat the olive oil. Fry the garlic and onion softly, stir occasionally for almost 3 minutes.
- Move the roasted vegetables into a casserole. Stir in the sliced tomatoes and the Provence spices. Flavor with the season. Switch heat to low, place on a cap, and allow for another ten minutes to cook.
- Clear entirely from the heat, and let it cool.
- Place the Roasted Ratatouille mix on parchment paper-covered dehydrator plates.

- Dehydrate for 10-12 hours at 63 ° C (145 ° F), until fully dry and brittle. Divide the mixture into three equal parts of the Roasted Ratatouille and put it into different zip lock containers.

One part to rehydrate

- Pour the dry Rotatouille mixture into a bowl, then add 1 cup of water.
- Take to a boil and simmer until it has rehydrated, stirring regularly for around 10 minutes.

Simple Seafood Curry

Ingredients:

- Dehydrated and cooked basmati rice1/4 cup
- 1/4 cup dehydrated seafood mix
-
- Dehydrated Thai curry paste 1 teaspoon.
  Powdered   tomato   sauce   2   Tbsps.
  Powdered coconut milk, 3 tbsps.

Instructions:

- Combine all the above-mentioned ingredients in a sealable plastic container that is medium in thickness.
- Pour dried curry mix into the saucepan and pour 1/4 cup sugar.
- Place the pot in a saucepan and bring to a boil on moderate heat.
- Allow to cook for 5 minutes, stirring every now and then turn off heat.
  Cover the pan for the next 10 minutes to allow the dish to cool completely.

Soba and Veggie Stir Fry
Ingredients:

- Dehydrated different bell peppers 2 tbsp.
- Dehydrated mushrooms 1 tbsp.
- About 60g/2 oz. Soba Buckwheat Noodles 1 Bundle
-
- *Note: Use gluten-free soy sauce or soba noodles in gluten free edition
- Freeze-dried beef mince 1/2 cup Chili sauce 1 Tsp.
- 1 tsp light gluten-free soy sauce Fish
  sauce 1 tsp.

Instructions:

- Add mushrooms and dehydrated vegetables in a zip lock container.
- All sauces should be placed in a small jar that is leak-proof.
-

Box individual soba noodles. Mix the dried mushrooms and vegetables in a bowl. Add 1 cup water.

- Place the pot and bring to a boil over moderate flame.
- Cook for approximately 5 minutes, stirring frequently.
-
- Cook the soba for 5 minutes.
-

Turn off the flame and drain the noodles. Mix the sauce well.

Chapter 5: Recipes of Desserts and Snacks Using Dehydrated Foods

The best snacks and desserts are made from dehydrated fruits and veggies. Dehydrated fruits and veggies can be used in regular dessert recipes as an alternative to fresh fruits and vegetable.

Asian countries are known for their dehydrated fruit snacks. They are a healthier option to chips, French fries, and nachos. These delicious recipes can be used to make desserts and snacks. You can also enjoy the full flavor of your favorite vegetable or fruit.

5.1 Recipes of Snacks

Beef Jerky
Ingredients:
- 0.66 lb. lean cut meat (beef) 300 grams
- Light soy sauce 1/2 cup
-
- Fresh squeezed orange juice 1/2 cup
- Minced garlic cloves, 2 Brown Sugar 1
- tbsp.

Fresh grated ginger 1 tsp.

Instructions:
- Cut off the extra fat and beef silver skin.
- The lean cut beef should be taken and stored in a freezer-friendly bag.

Freeze the meat for approximately 2 hours.
- Take the meat from the freezer and break into pieces of 3-6 mm (1/4"-1/8).
- Combine all of the marinade components into a pot.
- Marinate the beef and then combine well to coat each piece.
-
- Cook covered for 6-8 hours.
- Remove beef. Use a colander to drain.

Layer slices of beef on a dehydrator tray.

Dry for one hour at 160-165F/71-7CC. Then lower the temperature to 155F/68C. Finally, dry until pliable with no visible moisture patches (approximately 5-7hrs

Cinnamon Apple-Chips
Ingredients:
- Medium-size apple 4
- Sugar 1/4 cup
- Ground cinnamon 1 tbsp.

Instructions:

- Wash the apples, and core them.
- Cut apples into small circles between 1/8-1/4" (3-6 mm) wide using a mandolin or a steak knife.
- Combine cinnamon and sugar in a medium cup.
- Arrange the apple slices in a single layer on dehydrator mesh boards.
- Sprinkle the combination of sugar and cinnamon on sliced apples.
- Dehydrate for 10-12 hours at 57C/135F, before clean.
- Let them cool down at room temperature.
- Store in a quiet, cold spot in an airtight jar.

Instant Hummus

Ingredients:

- 400g/14oz rinsed and drained chickpeas 1 can
- Minced garlic clove, 1 Tahini 2 tbsps.
- Fresh juice of lemon 3 tbsps. Sea
- salt according to taste Paprika
- 1/2 tsp.
- Ground cumin 1/2 tsp.
- Water, 3 tbsps. and more according to the requirement
- Extra virgin olive oil for serving three packets
-

Instruction:

- Add all ingredients in a spice grinder, except for the olive oil.
- Combine until the paste is smooth.
- Pour additional water to achieve the target quality.
- Add salt flavor, and change when appropriate.
-

Place the hummus mixture on non-stick layer or parchment paper-lined dehydrator trays. Let it dehydrate for around 3-4 hours at 130 ° F/55 ° C, or until fully dry and crispy.

- Let chill to room temperature, and crush into a powder dehydrated hummus.
- Split dehydrated hummus into separate parts (roughly two heaped tbsps. apiece) and load them into sealable plastic bags of medium scale. Please place them in a nice, dark spot.

One part to rehydrate:

- In the container with the dried hummus, pour 2-3 tbsps. Of cold water and one tablespoon or one package of extra virgin olive oil.
- Place the bag and with your hands press. Knead it until well mixed. Savor
- with pita, flatbread, or bagel crackers.

Crackers and Hummus
Ingredients:
- Instant hummus mixture 2 tbsps.
- Olive oil one packet
- Low-carb crackers (any amount of your choice)

Instruction:

- In the container with the dried hummus, pour 2 to 3 tbsps. Of cold water and a single olive oil packet.
- Place the bag in your hands and press / knead it until well mixed. Enjoy
- hummus with crackers.

Smoky-Beer Beef Jerky
Ingredients:

- 1.54 lb. lean cut of beef, 700 grams
- 0.44l Guinness draught 1 can

Light soy sauce 1/2 cup Honey, 1
- tbsp.
- Liquid smoke 1 tbsp.
- Minced garlic, 2 cloves
- Ground black pepper according to taste or 1 tsp.

Instructions:

- Cut off any surplus fat and beef silver skin.
- Place the beef in a zip-lock pocket and freeze until solidified for around 2 hours.
- Take the meat from the freezer and split into pieces of 4-6 mm (1/4"-1/8).
- Mix all of the marinade components into a pot.
- Marinate the meat, then mix well to cover each piece.
- Cap and chill for 6-8 hours.
- Take out beef. Use a colander to drain.
- Put slices of beef on the dehydrate plate.
- Dry for 1 hour at 160-165F/71-74C, then lower temperature to 155F/68C and proceed to dry until flexible, with no noticeable moisture patches (approximately 4-6 hours).

Apple   Jerky

Ingredients:

- 796 ml Apple Sauce 28 oz. 1 jar
- Banana 1 chopped Dates,
- 6 79 ml Flax Seeds ⅓ Cup
- 30 ml Honey 2 Tbsp.
- 15 ml Agave Nectar 1 Tbsp.
- 15 ml Cinnamon 1 Tbsp.
- 118 ml Orange Juice ½ Cup

shredded apples, 2
- 236 ml uncooked Oatmeal, 1 Cup
- 118 ml shredded Coconut, ½ Cup
- 708 ml Krispy's Rice Cereal 3 Cups

Instructions:

- In a mixer, add sliced dates, apple sauce, honey, banana, flax, and cinnamon seeds. Let this stay to relax the dates while getting ready for the other stuff.
- Take two apples: Cut, core, and slice. Throughout a large mixing pot, blend with an orange drink.
- To prevent the apples from becoming brown, turn it about a little. Fill the mixing bowl with almond, oatmeal, and Rice Krispy's and whisk.
- Switch on the blender for almost 2 minutes, or before it is well mixed.
- Unload the contents of the blender into the bowl, and mix equally. Pour
- the mix into a full bag or a jerky gun. Cut 1/2 inch hole in one edge while carrying a pocket.
- Fill dehydrating trays with parchment paper or sheets.
- Keep apple jerky lined up on plates. When utilizing an Excalibur Dehydrator, they will make three trays.
- Dry for about nine hours, at 135 ° F. Switch off the paraflex sheets at five hours and start drying. Will dry leather like berries. Let the strips cool down and break into three or four bits. Walnut and Apricot Cookies Ingredients:

- Overnight soaked Walnuts 2 cups
- Sweet and sour fresh apricots or dried 1 cup
- Soaked Raisins 1 small cup
- Over-ripe bananas 2

Instructions:

- Use a blender to blend the batter to the crumby consistency and spoon out on any dehydrator tray.
- Dehydrate at a temperature of 105 F for 24 hours, or until dry (do not over dehydrate).
- Switch them over within 8-12 hours, or when one portion is dry enough.
- Experiment with the nuts, beans, and fruits you want. A mix of fresh fruit and a few dried, soaked fruits with nuts is also nice. You can use sunflower seeds for veggie/'salty crackers, and they appear to offer a salty taste when dry. You can, of course, include some other soaked nuts/seeds.

Raw Fruit Leather

They are great for making a fast and balanced snack while you're on the go. Hold some of those in the fridge for whenever you like to snack.

This recipe makes eight rolls of fruit leather, which can be quickly doubled or tripled to match your requirements. If you don't like raspberries, strawberries or blackberries are just as good going to work.

Ingredients:

- Banana 1
- Frozen or fresh raspberries 2 cups

Instructions:

- Puree the raspberries and bananas into a dense fruity mixture in your food processor, adding more water when required.
- If you may not like the seeds, use a strainer to strain the mixture before adding the banana.
- Next, coat the dehydrator plate with a light coating of coconut oil and fill it with fruit mix, using a spoon to ensure even distribution

- Dehydrate for 8 to 12 hours on 118 degrees or overnight.
- The resulting fruit leather should be pliable and not gluey.
  Split into eight pieces of similar thickness, then shape into funnel
  shapes

Fruit Leather
Ingredients:
- Pears 2 large
- Fuji apples 3 small
- Cinnamon 1 stick
Instructions:

- Wash the pears and oranges, remove seeds and dice.
- Place in a processor and add a tiny volume of filtered water and
cinnamon, for approximate thirty seconds processing. Pour mixture over
- teflex sheets and put dehydrator plates.
- Dehydrate for 6-8 hours, cut the teflex pads, and turn leather over the
berries.
- Continue to dehydrate before the required humidity is collected. Use
- any fruit and some combination to produce a fruit leather.

Apple Chips

These are fantastic snacking options. Children love these. The kind of grocery
store has sugar, among other unnecessary products, but homemade chips are
much healthier.

Peel the apples (if you want without apple skin), core and piece very thinly.
Lightly dust with cinnamon. In a dehydrator, dehydrate for about 6-8 hours
at 135 degrees until crunchy. Keep in airtight bins, and you won't consume
them all at once.

You can tie these on your Christmas tree for the kids to have as a treat
(instead of candy canes). You should attach these to the Christmas tree
mostly as a surprise for the kids (rather than candy canes).

Paleo Biscotti (based on Bliss Bars)

Mix the two styles of nuts: Almond-Cashew (cashew not GRAP), BrazilPine, or Sunflower-Date or Walnut-Datem sliced macadamias, any combination of nut/fruit/fruit you want, with just enough honey to hold together. If you wish you might mix in a few puffed amaranth OR, the almond flour, or arrowroot, could act as an "adhesive" to keep the bar intact. Then start making bars, about just the size of Kudos, and dehydrate for 12-24 hours at 100 degrees.

Kale Chips with Cashew Cheese Sauce Ingredients:

Cashew nut pieces 2 cups
- Carrot (optional) 1
- Red bell pepper 1/2 Nutritional
- yeast 6 tbsp.
- Sea salt 1/4 tsp.
- Lemon juice up to 2 tsp. or juice of one lemon
- Water 1 1/2 cups
- Kale 2 bunches [should be enough for a 9-tray Excalibur dehydrator]

Instructions:

- Divide the kale into manageable sections, and cut the main stem. In a big mixing pot, rinse. Mix all sauce components in a mixer. Place cashew cheese sauce over bits of kale and throw kale. Fix on sheets with a dehydrator and dehydrate at 135 for 2 hours, then at 115 for up to 5 or 6 hours until it is crispy. [It's not essential to be in such a hurry. 105 ° F will operate for 10 hours, too.]

Raw Kale Chips with Sundried Tomato Dressing
Ingredients:

- Washed and stems removed of kale, 1 bunch Dressing:
- Red pepper 1
- Any nut butter or tahini 1/3 cup
- Basil 1 cup
- Juice of a half lemon
- Oil removed sundried tomatoes, 4
- Sea salt or seasoning according to taste
- (optional)chili flakes or chili oil according to taste

Instructions:

- Mix all the dressing additives
- Spoon the sauce into the large bowl. Start the sauce, and then apply chili flakes if you want it extra spicier.
- Cut or tear the kale into bits, and press in your palms a little. Stir
- in the dressing and thoroughly blend.

Drying raw kale chips:

- Layer pieces of kale on the dehydrator plates.
- Set 135 degrees to the dehydrator and allow 6 hours to dry.

Baking kale chips:

- Set the oven to 350 Fahrenheit.
- Layer pieces of kale onto a baking tray.
- Bake for ten minutes until it is crunchy. If it switches color to brown, gets kale out instantly.

Time to Cook: 10 minutes.

Yields 3 freezer bag chip, so it's best to adjust the recipe double or triple the process. A double recipe will fit into Excalibur 9 plate dehydrator, and it would involve dehydration for 7 hours.]

Nacho Cheese Kale Chips

Ingredients:

- Curly kale 1 head
- Macadamia nuts, 1 cup, soaked in water for at least 20 minutes
- Bell pepper 1
- Cayenne pepper according to taste
- Sea salt according to taste

Instructions:

- Split the kale into bits away from the stem, rinse and put aside.
- Rinse bell pepper and break it into large pieces.
- Process Bell pepper and macadamia nuts in blender with a touch of cayenne pepper and sea salt. Blend and adjust the taste. Sea salt and cayenne pepper can be balanced according to taste.
- Unless the sauce is too dense, you might need to add a little bit of water.

Spinach Crackers

Ingredients:

- Spinach rinsed and dried 3 pounds (or any other leafy green vegetable)
- Sea salt 1/2 tsp.
- Allspice 1/4 tsp.
- Curry powder 1/4 tsp.

(You can mix and combine different spices for a distinct flavor)

Instructions:

- Push all the ingredients into a food processor or blender.
- Layer into a food dehydrator, and use the fruit leather paper.
- Dry through the night.
- It will be crisply dehydrated in the morning, based on the water content of the spinach.
- Split it in bits, and store it in an airtight jar.

Fried Onions

These types of fried onions are an outstanding complement to soups and salads. Furthermore, they're going to perfectly preserve in the freezer, so produce extra, and you're going to have them for a while.

Ingredients:

- Onions 3 lbs.
- Sunflower seeds 1 cup, soak in water for 4 to 6 hours
- Red pepper 1/2
- Nutritional yeast 2 tbsp.
- Olive oil 1 tbsp.
- Lemon juice 1 tbsp. Tahini
- 1 tbsp.
- Garlic clove 1/2
Sea salt according to taste

Instructions:

- Cut the onions around 1/4-1/2 "long.
- Sauce: Mix the leftover ingredients in a blender. Process until smooth.
- Put onions on a teflex dehydrator tray or baking surface.
- Dehydrate until crunchy for almost 24 hours. Use the lowest temperature for preparing, and then roast until crisp.

Rosemary Sweet Potato Chips

Sweet potatoes should not have to be baked until they are consumed, unlike white potatoes. You can season these nutritious chips with rosemary, though some dried ingredients, such as onion powder, garlic powder, nutritional yeast, cayenne pepper or paprika, may be substituted.

Ingredients

- Sweet potato 1 large Olive
- oil 2 tbs.
- Lemon juice 1 tbs.
- Dried crushed rosemary, 1 tsp. Sea
- salt 1/2 tsp.

Instructions:

- Slice the sweet potato into thin pieces of paper with a sharp knife or mandolin.
- Put pieces in a cup and rub softly until well covered in lemon juice and oil.
- Add salt and rosemary, and combine to toss.
- Place pieces, without touching, on dehydrator plates.
- Dehydrate for almost 8 to 10 hours or transfer trays as required for even drying of chips until crunchy.
- Switch off the dehydrator, and absolutely cool the chips. Place several weeks in an airtight bag.

Carrot Pulp Crackers

Ingredients:

- Golden flaxseeds 1/2 cup
- Water at room temperature 1 cup
- About 2 medium tomatoes (chopped, raw, ripe,) 1 cup Lemon
- juice freshly squeezed 1 tbsp.
- Carrot pulp 3 cups.
- Salt 1 tsp or according to your taste.

Instructions:

- In a big tub, combine the flaxseeds in water and soak when all the water is absorbed around four hours.
- When flaxseed is prepared, process the lemon juice, tomato, and salt in a blender until liquid.
- Add carrot pulp to the tub. Mix carefully. If it is too hot, put a bit of water.
- Place a specified tablespoon of pulp mix on non-stick dehydrator pads, and push softly down to mold and shape circular crackers with the slotted spoon.
- Dehydrate for at least 6 to 10 hours at 105 degrees F (you can do it overnight). Turn the crackers forward, cut the sheet, and bring on the mesh layer directly.
- Dehydrate until crispy (some more than 6 hours). Stop
- and serve. Store in an airtight jar.

Ranch Carrot Chips

Ingredients

- CARROTS4 LARGE
- RANCH SEASONING 1 TBSP., HOMEMADE, OR PACKET ARE SUITABLE.
- SALT AND PEPPER ACCORDING TO TASTE
- WATER OR FRESH JUICE OF A LEMON TO MAKE STICKS OF HERBS

Instructions

- RINSE AND PEEL CARROTS. SLICE CARROTS IN HALF AND THEN THINLY SLICE THEM INTO SEGMENTS USING A MANDOLIN.
- PUT CARROTS TO DISH AND COVER, SPRINKLE WITH GRAIN, SALT & PEPPER. BASED ON HOW DRIED THE CARROTS ARE, LEMON JUICE/WATER CAN BE REQUIRED TO ALLOW THE SEASONING TO ADHERE.
- PLACE SLICES ON DEHYDRATOR PLATES TO ENSURE THAT THEY HAVE AMPLE ROOM AND DO NOT STRIKE.
- Dehydrate for 8-10 hours, at 115 f. When dehydrated completely, carrots must be crispy and hard. Place in an airtight jar.

Sun-dried Tomato and Cheesy Kale Chips Ingredients:

- Kale, (without stems discarded with diced leaves) 1 large bunch Organic
- sundried-tomatoes 30 grams, dipped in water to soak for at least 1 hour
- Raw cashews 1 cup, submerged in water to soak for at least 1 hour
- Garlic cloves 2 large
- Soaked water of tomatoes 3/4 cup plus 2 tbsp.
- Fresh basil 3-4 tbsp.
- Juice of fresh lemon 2 tbsp.
- Nutritional yeast2 tbsp.
- Fine grain sea salt 3/4 tsp., or according to taste

Instructions:

- Drench the sundried tomatoes and cashew nuts in water in 2 different bowls for at least an hour, but ideally at least 1.5-2 hours if necessary.
- Reserve the tomato dipping water until drying, then put aside. Strain the cashews, then rinse.
- Add garlic in a food processor, running the machine, and process until it is minced.

- Dump the remaining ingredients, excluding the oil. Cycle until smooth, scrap edges as needed, and then gradually add salt according to taste. Rinse the leaves of the kale and cut the kale into parts, then remove the roots. Secure the leaves in a spinner for salad (this makes the sauce stick).
- Put greens in a medium bowl. Spill the cheese sauce over the kale, then stir with a spatula. Then throw the spoon to bring your hands in there to rub the sauce onto the kale until it is fully covered. Dress with to taste oil.
- Dehydrate at 105–110F for about 12 hours. Once they're super crisp, kale chips are finished, and taste amazing.

Baked Cucumber-Chips

Ingredients
- Cucumbers or 2 medium or 3 small Avocado
- oil or olive oil 1 tbsp.
- Apple cider vinegar 2 tsp. or any vinegar of choice (if using regular chips, omit vinegar)
- Sea salt 1/2 tsp. or add more if required

Instructions

- Cut cucumber in very thin slices. You can use a mandolin cutter for better results.
- Use a paper towel to clear the extra moisture from cuts.
- Place the cucumber pieces in a big bowl and add vinegar, butter, and salt to mix.

To dehydrate:
- Place chunks on plates and dehydrate for 10-12 hours at 125-135 ° F or until crunchy.

For oven: Put slices on a baking tray lined with parchment. Dry 3-4 hours at 175 ° F, or until crunchy. Let the slices cool down before eating.

Raw Dehydrated Mexican Crackers
Ingredients
- Golden flaxseeds 1 cup
- Raw sunflower seeds 1/2 cup
- Fresh pumpkin seeds 1/2 cup
- Chia seeds 1/2 cup
- Diced yellow onion, 1/4
- Diced red bell pepper, 1/4
- Carrot 1 cup and leftover celery pulp from juicing Chipotle
- powder 1 1/2 tsp.
- Garlic powder 1 tsp.
- Celtic sea salt 1 tsp.

Cayenne pepper 1/2 tsp.

Instructions

- Put the flax, sunflower seeds, chia, and pumpkin seeds in different cups. Cover with water any meal, and enable to soak for around 6 hours.
- Pour the flax and chia with sufficient water to form it into a gel. For every bowl, it's about 1 cup.
- Wash and strain the sunflower seeds and pumpkin seeds.
- Toss onion and bell pepper in a food processor equipped with the sharp blade and process until it is almost a fluid consistency.
- Add the washed seeds of sunflower and pumpkin, garlic powder, the juice pulp, and chipotle powder, cayenne, and salt, and finish well together. Mix through the gels of chia and flax until blended well. Scrape the blend out

and layer over mesh dehydrator plates equipped with non-stick sheets in even slender (1/8th-inch) layers.

- Using a sharp tool like a pizza cutter or knife to shape the layers crackers into the form and scale you might want.
- Set your 115 ° F dehydrator, and dehydrate for around six hours. Remove the non-stick sheets and flip the cracker pieces onto the mesh screens directly and dehydrate for another 6 hours or until totally dry and crunchy.
- Place in a jar with seal.

Onion Nut Dehydrated Crackers

Ingredients

- Sunflower crispy seeds 1 cup
- Crispy cashews 1 cup
- Water ½ cup
- Coconut amino ¼ cup or tamari
- Green onion 1 large
- Garlic clove 1 large

Instructions

- Transfer all components to a food processor, and mix until well mixed.
- Cover one parchment paper dehydrator tray (or using Teflex).
- Layer mixture to coat both boards. Lay a further parchment paper on its top and use a rolling pin to roll out, if the blend is moist and tight to spread. Dry for around an hour at 115 for fresh crackers, and then decrease to 105 for.
- When you're not worried about having the cookies raw, feel free to raise the temperature. No matter the level, make sure to share the crackers in the dehydrator after around an hour.
- Bring the timer down! To shape the grid, use a knife or pizza slicer. It would make things that are more straightforward to smash the end product into crackers when needed.

- Dehydrate until dry, crispy, and cracker-like. The dry period can differ considerably. It all refers to the amount of humidity in your household, the dehydrator heat, the cracker mix dampness, and so on.
- You can turn the large sheet of crackers around 6 hours later to speed things up. At this time, cut the parchment leaf.
- Don't overthink about dehydrating them out. Ensuring they are thoroughly dry and crunchy is safer than getting them out too long and winding up with soft cookies.
- Place in a dry jar, which is airtight.

Fried and Dried Siracha Chickpeas

Ingredients
- Can of chickpeas 19-ounce, 1 Sriracha
- 3 tbsp.
- Salt 1 tsp.
- Sugar 1 tbsp.

Instructions
- Put the chickpeas on a kitchen towel and rinse well with a soft hand.
- Drop the salt and sriracha into a wide pot. Attach the chickpeas and garnish equally.
- Toss with the sugar and move to a fruit dehydrator tray lined with a fruit tray. Set for 10-12 hours at 130 degrees, and then dehydrate. Add a bit of olive oil over medium-low heat to a saute pan to saute them. Place only for a minute or two in a reasonable number of chickpeas, tossing the pan to avoid scorching. Offer warm or at room temperature.

Granola Recipe

Ingredients:

- Cooked buckwheat, 2 cups
- Rolled oats raw 1 cup
- Apples 3
- Dried cranberries 1 cup, or raisins
- Dried apple slices 1 cup, or other dried fruit
- Dates (pits removed) 30, dipped in water to soak for 15 minutes (you can add more if you want sweeter snacks)
- Raw almonds 1 cup
- Raw sunflower seeds 1 1/4 cups Honey
- 1/2 cup
- Cinnamon 1 tsp. Sea
- salt 1 tsp.

Instructions:

- Place 1 cup of buckwheat cooked in a food processor, cored apples (hold the peel), dates, cinnamon, honey, salt, and 1/4 cup sunflower seeds.
- Crush until smooth. Measure the mixture into a large mixing pot. Add
- 1/2 cup almonds, 1/4 cup sunflower seeds, dried apple slices, 1/2 cup cranberries, (or other fruits) to the spice grinder (you don't have to rinse the bowl between these steps). Chop the seeds, nuts, and fruit rather coarsely in a few short pulses.
- Add the apple mix to the pot, and blend properly.
- Add the oats and remaining almonds, buckwheat, cranberries, and sunflower seeds, in the blend and mix.
- If the mixture is too cold, apply one more drop of oats to the mix. The dough is expected to be sticky but not runny. The different degrees of chopped seeds, nuts, and fruits offer a stunning texture to this granola.

Put the granola dough on cling film to turn into 1/2 inch thick bars and then cut into 4 inch long pieces.

- Optionally, use a biscuit cutter to form the granola dough into no-bake oatmeal cookies-ideal for lunch and snacks for children.
- Put the granola bars or biscuits on dehydrator plates and dehydrate for 4 hours at 135 degrees. Turn the bars back and start to dry for the next hour, based on how tangy and soft the granola bars you like.
- If you chose very crispy granola bars, then continue to dehydrate for another eight hours.
- Place in an airtight jar until it has cooled down thoroughly.
- Keep in the fridge for up about a week to hold freshness longer.

Raw Dehydrated Corn Chips

Ingredients:

- Frozen corn 4 cups (defrosted)
- Roughly chopped and de-seeded yellow bell pepper 1 Apple
- cider vinegar 2 tbsps.
- Flaxseed ground ½ cup Salt 2
- tsp.
- Water ¼ cup or 1/2 cup depending on the thickness

Instructions

- Dump all ingredients (leaving the linseed/flax) in a blender or food processor and process until smooth,
- Now dump the flax, and then blend until thoroughly blended.
- Distribute the batter between the two sheets of the non-stick dehydrator, and mold in the shape you want.
- Dehydrate for 8-10 hours at 115F, turn onto a mesh plate and dehydrate for another 12 hours or until it is crisp. Keep for several weeks in an airtight bag.

Dehydrated Kiwi Chips

- Remove the skin from kiwi. You can use a spoon to insert under the skin directly and then twist the kiwi, trying to keep the spoon towards the skin surface.
- Similarly, you may use a sharp knife or a potato peeler to take the skin away.
- Slice the skinned kiwis into 6 mm (1/4) fillets.
- Put on a dehydrator pad and dehydrate for 6-12 hours at 135 ° F (37 ° C). You should even put these on a baking sheet in the oven at the least temperature if you don't have a dehydrator, testing them after around 4 hours because an oven appears to be hotter. When done, those should be mildly chewy.

5.2 Recipes of Desserts

<u>Chocolate Almond Smoothie</u>
Ingredients:
- Banana 1
- Rolled oats or wheat berries 2 tbsps.
- Peanut butter or almond butter 1 tbsp.
- Ground flaxseed 1 tsp. Cocoa
- powder 1 tsp.
- Almond milk 3/4 cup

Instructions:
- Add all ingredients together in a blender.
- Blend at high-speed cycle before smooth and frothy.
- Distribute over dehydrator plate coated with a sheet of non-stick or parchment paper.
- Dehydrate for 6-12 hours at 115F/46C, until thoroughly dried and hard.
- Take them out and allow cool to room temperature.
- Grind the dried smoothie blend into a powder form in a coffee grinder.
- Store in a tiny zip lock container.
- Spill the smoothie powder into a cup or a large bottle.
- Mix/stir well and pour 2/3 cup water.
- Let sit to rehydrate for 5–10 minutes. Stir and relax again.

<u>Mango Coconut Smoothie</u>
Ingredients:

- Mango chunks (frozen) 1 cup
- Gluten-free rolled oats, 2 tbsps.
- Shredded coconut (unsweetened) 2 tbsps. Coconut
- milk 3/4 cup

Instructions:

- Add all the above-mentioned ingredients together in a blender or food processor.
- Blend at high-speed cycle before smooth and frothy.
- Distribute over dehydrator plate coated with a sheet of non-stick or parchment paper.
- Dehydrate for 6-12 hours at 115F/46C, until thoroughly dried and hard.
- After dehydrating, let it cool to room temperature.
- Grind the dried smoothie blend into a powder form in a spice grinder.
- Fit into a small zip-lock pocket.
- Spill the smoothie mix into a mug or a large bottle.
- Mix/squish well and add 2/3 cup water.
- Let sit to rehydrate for 5–10 minutes. Mix thoroughly.

Angel Cake
Ingredients:
- Dehydrated strawberry slices½ cup Dehydrated
- angel food-cake crumbs 1 cup Sweetened
- cocoa-powder 3 tbsp.
- Water ½ cup plus a few teaspoons

Instructions:

- Dehydrate angel food cake in 1/2 inch chunks then cut in smaller bits afterward.

- Load dried strawberries in two little plastic bags and a sweetened cocoa blend. Chocolate powdered milk also works well.
- Cover a dried angel food cake entirely in a large plastic bag.

- Mix the strawberries in a bowl of water. Power stove and steam it over low heat for 10 minutes. The goal is to rehydrate and heat the strawberries, while at the same time making some delicious strawberry juices, not to cook out the red ones.
- In a separate bowl, mix the cocoa powder with four teaspoons of water. Transfer strawberries and liquids to a filling cup if you use one saucepan and make the chocolate sauce in the same pan. Stir properly over low heat until the sauce hits the perfect strength, pouring more water a spoonful at a time.
- Layer with cake crumbs over the strawberries. Move the cake deep into the juices for the strawberry, but don't mix. Drizzle over the cake with chocolate sauce. Most of the cake will consume the juices from the strawberry, and others will stay crunchy. Try by spooning.

Peach Cobbler

Ingredients:
- Dried peach slices, ½ cup
- Bread crumbs ¼ cup Sugar
- 2 tsp.
- Nutmeg 1 pinch
- Water ½ cup

Instructions:

- Load a small plastic bag with dried sugar, peaches, and nutmeg. Seal up in a bigger plastic container with the bread crumbs to remain packed.

You might use simple Italian-style loaf for making the bread crumbs, or you can use dried flatbread for more of a pie-crust quality.

- Mix dried sugar, peach, and nutmeg with water. Power stove and steam it over low heat for 10 minutes—no need to simmer-you want to rehydrate and steam the peaches.
- Take the mix off from the stove, and mix in the crumbs of bread. The bread crumbs will absorb the light peach juices.

Apple Pie

Ingredients:
- Dried apple slices, ½ cup
- Bread crumbs ½ cup
- Raisins ¼ cup Sugar 2
- tsp.
- Cinnamon ¼ tsp. Water
- ½ cup

Instructions:

- Load a small plastic bag with dried sugar, apples, cinnamon and raisin. Seal up in a bigger plastic container with the bread crumbs to remain packed.
- You might use simple Italian-style loaf for making the bread crumbs, or you can use dried flatbread for more of a pie-crust quality.
- Mix dried sugar, apple, cinnamon and raisins with water. Power stove and steam it over low heat for 10 minutes—no need to simmer-you want to rehydrate and steam the peaches.
- Take the mix off from the stove, and mix in the crumbs of bread. The bread crumbs will absorb the light peach juices.

Banana Nut Bread Pudding

Ingredients:

- Dried banana slices, ½ cup
- Mixed nuts ¼ cup Dried
- bread crumbs ¼ cup Sugar
- 2 tsp.
- Water ½ cup

Instructions:

For a Larger Portion: The recipe below contains 364 calories. Use 1⁄3 cup of mixed nuts, 3⁄4 cup of dried bananas, 1⁄3 cup of dried bread crumbs, 3⁄4 cup of water and 3 tsp. of sugar to rehydrate to form a larger size with 504 calories.

- The bread crumbs for this recipe are pieces, not ground.
- Mix dried bananas and potted sugar with warm water. Power stove and steam it over low heat for 10 minutes. Without any need to boil – heat up and rehydrate the banana.
- Stir in the bread crumbs and nuts and turn off the stove. The bread crumbs will absorb the sweet juices, and the bananas break into a custard form.

Printed in Great Britain
by Amazon

27727936R00063